Mental Disorders in Popular Film

Mental Disorders in Popular Film

How Hollywood Uses, Shames, and Obscures Mental Diversity

Erin Heath

LEXINGTON BOOKS
Lanham • Boulder • New York • London

Published by Lexington Books
An imprint of The Rowman & Littlefield Publishing Group, Inc.
4501 Forbes Boulevard, Suite 200, Lanham, Maryland 20706
www.rowman.com

6 Tinworth Street, London SE11 5AL

Copyright © 2019 by The Rowman & Littlefield Publishing Group, Inc.

All rights reserved. No part of this book may be reproduced in any form or by any electronic or mechanical means, including information storage and retrieval systems, without written permission from the publisher, except by a reviewer who may quote passages in a review.

British Library Cataloguing in Publication Information Available

Library of Congress Cataloging-in-Publication Data

Names: Heath, Erin, author.
Title: Mental disorders in popular film : how Hollywood uses, shames, and obscures mental diversity / Erin Heath.
Description: Mental disorders in popular film : how Hollywood uses, shames, and obscures mental diversity / Erin Heath.
Identifiers: LCCN 2018057402 (print) | LCCN 2019000348 (ebook) | ISBN 9781498521727 (electronic) | ISBN 9781498521710 (cloth : alk. paper) | ISBN 9781498521734 (pbk. : alk. paper)
Subjects: LCSH: Mental illness in motion pictures. | Motion pictures--United States--History and criticism.
Classification: LCC PN1995.9.M463 (ebook) | LCC PN1995.9.M463 H43 2019 (print) | DDC 791.43/6561--dc23
LC record available at https://lccn.loc.gov/2018057402

∞™ The paper used in this publication meets the minimum requirements of American National Standard for Information Sciences Permanence of Paper for Printed Library Materials, ANSI/NISO Z39.48-1992.

Printed in the United States of America

Contents

Acknowledgments — vii
Introduction — 1

1 Gender and Reality in *Fight Club* and *Black Swan* — 11
2 Villainizing and Psychopaths in *The Dark Knight* and *The Silence of the Lambs* — 29
3 Cognitive Theory and Autism in *Rain Man* and *Mary and Max* — 41
4 Disability Theory and Race in *Radio* and *The Soloist* — 55
5 Institutionalization and Gaslighting in *Girl, Interrupted* and *12 Monkeys* — 69

Conclusion — 85
Bibliography — 89
Index — 93
About the Author — 97

Acknowledgments

The research and writing of this book have been greatly supported by my family and friends. I would like to thank my parents for the unending faith that they have always shown in me. Anne and Gary Heath have never let me think that I wasn't completely capable of anything that I sought, and apparently, I have come to believe them. I appreciate the moral support of my siblings, Amy Hensley, Kristen Heath, and Mike Hensley, for listening when I did talk about it, but not pressuring when I didn't; and Retha Pritchett, my grandmother, for always being a comfort and a resource.

I greatly appreciate my friends and colleagues who have cheered me on and offered much-needed support, especially Melissa Kennedy, Dr. Rebecca West, Dr. Maria O'Connell, Dr. Karen Beth Strovas, and Dr. Laura Brandenburg. You may not always know the ways that you helped, but believe that you did.

I would also like to thank my editors, Lindsey Falk, for believing in this idea from the start; and Judith Lakamper, who helped me get to the finish line.

Thanks.

Introduction

Contemporary Hollywood films commonly use mental disorders as a magnifier by which social, political, or economic problems become enlarged in order to critique societal conditions. These characters act violently out of anger, feel all-consuming love, and show overwhelming sadness. Cinema has a long history of amplifying human emotion or experience for dramatic effect. The heightened representations of people with mental disorder often elide one category of literal truths for the benefit of different moral or emotional reasons. In cinema, these selective choices frequently come at the expense of realistic representations of people with mental disorders. These characters also commonly become subject to the structures of hierarchy and control that actual people with mental disorders encounter. Cinematic patterns of control and oppression heavily influence the narratives of those considered "crazy" by the outside world.

I will address characters identified by film or media as people who are crazy, mentally ill, developmentally delayed, insane, have dissociative identity disorder (commonly known as multiple personality disorder), borderline personality disorder, psychotic disorders, antisocial personality disorder (commonly known as sociopathy or psychopathy), developmental disorder, anorexia, autism spectrum disorder (ASD), and other non-diagnosed or compounded conditions. I will most commonly use the term "people with a mental disorder," because the frame that I use for determining a person's inclusion in this remarkably varied group arises from the *Diagnostic and Statistical Manual of Mental Disorders: Fifth Edition*. As the *DSM-5* clearly establishes mental disorder as an inclusive diagnostic term, it is the term that I use most. Throughout the book, I use the *DSM-5*, not clinically as I am not a psychologist, but to establish my critical parameters and to clarify terms. I include such a broad range of characters because my object is to write as inclusively as possible in my discussion of these problematic representations. I do not equate all of these mental disorders in real people as one common lived experience. I do equate many of these films and some of their representations of people with a mental disorder. Despite the vast array of differences in people's experiences, film marginalizes people with mental disorders in ways that make it important to be inclusive of these varied experiences.

Similarly, I will most commonly use the term "normate" to provide a descriptor for a person without a diagnosable disorder. This applies to the characters in film that do not obviously or clearly demonstrate mental disorder. The term normate comes from Rosemarie Garland Thomson's book *Extraordinary Bodies: Figuring Physical Disability in American Culture and Literature*.[1] She describes the term as one that "usefully designates the social figure through which people can represent themselves as definitive human beings. Normate, then, is the constructed identity of those who, by way of the bodily configuration and cultural capital they assume, can step into a position of authority and wield the power it grants them. . . . What emerges is a very narrowly defined profile that describes only a minority of actual people."[2] The term "normate" avoids the terms "ordinary" or "normal," which presumes an identifiable standard of measure between those that are "normal" and those that would, in turn, be "abnormal." I integrate some of her language about disability and base some of my broader approach on her foundational theory; in much the same way that race is a social construct that informs social interactions and significance, Thomson examines how expectation, social constructs, bias, and the accessibility of space and architecture inform people's experiences of their differences. While she focuses on physical difference, I lean heavily on this interpretation and conceptualization of people with mental disorders who face similar stigma. According to Jayci Robb and Jeff Stone in their article "Implicit Bias toward People with Mental Illness: A Systematic Literature Review" in the *Journal of Rehabilitation*, "For example, participants were more likely to associate stimuli resembling 'dangerous' and 'bad' with mental illness than with physical illness."[3] This marks the importance of including mental difference in an examination of disability studies.

This book operates as a work of film criticism examining cinematic texts that share the single central conceit that one or more of the primary characters experiences some variety of mental disorder. Many film representations of people with mental disorder inform upon a variety of social, political, and critical theories either unrelated to mental disorder or problematically depicted alongside it. Robb and Stone also assert in their article that "Three of the most common stereotypes have included beliefs that people with mental illness are dangerous (e.g., Corrigan et al., 2002), incompetent (e.g., Sadler, Meagor, & Kaye, 2012), and responsible for the onset and offset of their condition. . . ."[4] These misunderstandings create fear and anxiety for many normates, and I argue that the presence of mental illness operates as a justification for the subjugation of the person with a mental disorder and thus establishes an excuse for oppression parallel to other issues, such as their social, political, racial, or sexual rebellion. In an effort to demonstrate the implications of representation on a broad range of people with mental disorder, I will examine a similarly expansive array of portrayals.

In my examination of these representations of people with mental disorder, I employ various theoretical approaches such as gender theory, theories of class and social inequality, and theories addressing institutional power. Disability studies is shaped by many of these same theories surrounding gender, race, and other representations. This work operates with my understanding that featuring several different theoretical approaches can shed light on diverse ways that films generally represent and reaffirm oppression of people with mental disorder. This book is a work of disability theory that samples numerous theoretical approaches including other disability theory. I feature a series of case studies underlying this multifaceted approach to disability studies. I argue that these varied theories alternately become relevant to explicating how film exploits representations of people with mental disorder to validate the punishment or control imposed by the expectations of the cinematic narrative.

Stephen Harper's *Madness, Power and the Media: Class, Gender and Race in Popular Representations of Mental Distress* and Simon Cross's *Mediating Madness: Mental Distress and Cultural Representation* both discuss the inaccuracies of many representations of people with mental disorders.[5] While perhaps not surprising, these authors agree that mental disorder does not generally appear in ways that demonstrate real people's lived experiences. Films like *Fight Club* and *Black Swan,* for example, intentionally make psychological breakdowns immediate and narratively convenient to provide audiences with an entertaining emotional struggle.

Primarily concerned with nonfiction representations especially in Great Britain, Simon Cross's *Mediating Madness* examines many of the complex and sometimes exploitive and negative representations of people with mental disorder. Cross's discussion of imagery works through paintings, photography, and ultimately documentary or other nonfiction television depictions. He uses the term madness as he looks at the concept of mental disorder largely in the ways that it becomes depicted in the media or popular perception rather than people's personal lived experiences of it. While mentioning a few fiction films, Cross does not focus his text on them, nor are the films as extensively examined as what I will do here.

Stephen Harper's *Madness, Power and the Media* also focuses largely on British media with the inclusion of only a few American texts. It similarly spends a significant period on television and print media as well as a few cinematic representations. Like Cross's work, because of the broad approach to the topic of madness and its representation, the discussion of films appears occasionally and does not function as his primary focus. His address of people with mental disorder also excludes people with what he articulates as "congenital mental disorders" or "psychopathy."[6] He does make an important point in this position as he elucidates the conflation of psychopathy and psychosis, which tends to imply that people with mental disorder are "ruthlessly immoral."[7] While Harper does address many of the same points of oppression and representation, his different national perspective, his broader address of varied media, and his more narrow focus of mental disorder construct a largely distinct set of narratives being addressed. His work also does not invest as much in close textual analysis or spend as much time invested in the intersection of these representations with gender or race.

In much the same way that Cross addresses a large array of kinds of representational texts, Stuart Murray in *Representing Autism: Culture, Narrative, Fascination*[8] looks at an array of representations from the news, books, the internet, and film. Murray covers autism spectrum disorder's recent shifts from obscurity to its more recent popular portrayals. He has an extensive discussion of *Rain Man* and other cinematic, literary, and media depictions of people with autism spectrum disorder. Cross's focus is useful for elucidating the particular biases that come with a recently popularized syndrome and its historical rise to the popular consciousness.

With the breadth and range of mental conditions encompassing a vast number of people and realities, I want to clarify that this book does not attempt to address, define, or explain actual lived mental disorders directly, but rather the American Hollywood film industry's representation of people that our culture labels as mad, crazy, mentally disabled, mentally ill, or broken. I am not a psychologist, nor is this an attempt to write a psychology textbook about the accuracy of these representations. Those books addressing the realism of cinema's depictions of people with mental disorders have been written. As mentioned above, Harper's book discusses the lack of correlation between actual lived mental disorder and cinematic representation. Instead, I analyze the methods behind these films' use of the trope of madness for creating narratives that actually invest in other issues about controlling characters who reject conformity, confront people in power, or who operate as outliers, especially those who confront social issues such as gender inequality, class dynamics, racial representation, and institutional gaslighting. *Fight Club* (1999) is a classic example of a film that features a character with multiple personality disorder, but the narrative primarily engages with issues of modern capitalistic masculinity.[9] This film shows little regard for a factual representation of mental health. While inaccurate representations in filmmaking frequently occur, these depictions raise issues about what these films communicate, how they use mental difference, and how they feature these conditions if accurate representation is not the primary concern.[10] I parse these various topics throughout the course of the book.

Due to the volume and diversity of representations of mental disorder, I can in no way cover all films on the subject. Thousands of films inside and outside Hollywood have characters that appear either overtly or implicitly like a person with a mental disorder. This book does not serve as an encyclopedic work, but rather a series of case studies examining the theoretical implications of representing a person with a mental disorder. Each chapter primarily addresses two different films that represent a particular issue or social construct in order to illustrate how people with a mental disorder are depicted and how films use it to elide their punishment or control over social outliers, minorities, or women.

The reasons for cinema's oppressive representation of people with a mental disorder stem from several social and cultural parameters. I argue in this book that one of those pressures is the history of the American Hollywood studio system. Hollywood cinema's representation of characters with mental disorder operates under the obligations and expectations of American moviegoers, cinematic tradition, cultural expectations, and historical movements. I discuss the ways that Hollywood cinema follows patterns in representing people with a mental disorder, and their implied obligations as shaped by cultural, social, and monetary pressures. For decades these moral parameters have fallen under the office of the Motion Picture Producers and Distributers of America (MPPDA), then the Production Code Administration (PCA) office more commonly known as the Hays Office, and now from the Motion Picture Association of America (MPAA).[11] According to Gregory D. Black in *Hollywood Censored: Morality Codes, Catholics, and the Movies*, the Hays office controlled which films found distribution and shaped how directors told their stories through voluntary censorship in order to avoid legal governmental censorship.[12] In more contemporary times the MPAA dictates ratings for films, which can greatly influence their profits. According to Kia Afra in her article about contemporary ratings, ". . . for Hollywood executives, the most economically viable rating is still PG-13 and not R. In the MPAA's demographic calculations, PG-13 is crucial for reaching the under 17 age group, which accounts for roughly 25 percent of the theatrical audience and, moreover, has profound effects on the movie choices of parents and guardians."[13] Due to these pressures, the Hays codes and the current MPAA have established a set of moral parameters that shape storytelling in Hollywood to this day. According to Black, under the Hays codes, evil characters typically suffer punishment, and the good experience triumph over the Other, which in some films means a person with a mental disorder.

The Other and Otherness can be defined as a cultural category of difference. Simone de Beauvoir in *The Second Sex* states "Otherness is a fundamental category of human thought. Thus it is that no group ever sets itself up as the One without at once setting up the Other over against itself."[14] This division of identities operates as part of the social and cultural divisions of power, authority, and control. The Other becomes a figure that does not fit into the dominant cultural categories of a particular space. Moira Gatens clarifies in her discussion of Otherness, "Power Bodies and Difference," "The crux of the issue of difference as it is understood here is that difference does not have to do with biological 'facts' so much as with the manner in which culture marks bodies and creates specific conditions in which they live and recreate themselves."[15] The term, "Other" includes people who do not conform to the dominant culture's expectations of race, class, gender, ability, or other socially accepted category and thus are subject to the dominant culture's oppressive structures. I will argue that in the last thirty years, the Motion Picture Association of America has continued to reflect some historical cinematic expectations about the Other that results in furthering the oppression and subjugation of people with a mental disorder.

I assert that the rules and parameters associated with the Hays codes and the traditions of American social conformity in film have created a kind of cinematic pattern. This trend does not mandate that necessarily all film conforms to its expectations, like punishing the villain, but rather that film history, tradition, and American expectations create great pressure to adapt to a relatively narrow set of moral standards; and I will show how this functions in these particular films and demonstrates these claims through intersectional theoretical approaches addressing people with disabilities, people of color, and women. These cinematic expectations commonly result in films reestablishing social norms, punishing certain kinds of outliers, and oppressing—sometimes overtly, sometimes subtly—the Other.

When exploring the issue of representation of mental disorder on film, I have encountered several different areas of critical concern, which I will address: concerns about gender identity, violence and criminality, cognitive identification, racial representation, and institutional gaslighting. These categories or loci became the core topics that I discuss. I then picked films that particularly highlighted the issues I was looking to investigate. When choosing films addressing these areas, I focused on a few criteria. These included the accessibility of the films, so that readers could easily access these texts through common approaches such as Amazon or Netflix. I also wanted to provide films that were largely although not exclusively indicative of the contemporary American Hollywood studio system or, in one case, in contrast to it. Then I looked for films that demonstrated a particular mental health diagnosis such as autism spectrum disorder, antisocial personality disorder (sociopaths), or dissociative identity disorder (multiple personality disorder). I paired types of disorders; because of the huge disparity in representations, a character with autism spectrum disorder and a character with dissociative identity disorder might have very little in common. For most chapters, I pair similar conditions in ways that help illustrate a particular concern as it is demonstrated in the work. This might include the ways that narratives with characters with autism spectrum disorders frequently concern themselves with social interactions; for example, *Mozart and the Whale, Adam,* or *The Good Doctor* frequently engage with the white heterosexual male characters' success or challenges with dating.[16] In films with people who have antisocial personality disorder, they frequently commit serial murders. Finally, I choose works that pair well to illustrate contrasts in representations of similar issues such as institutionalization or race. Some categories such as antisocial personality disorder have dozens of films that could be discussed while others, such as films with main characters who are both African American and have a mental disorder, occur exceedingly rarely in American cinema.

Among more common types of films, I choose works that were especially exemplary of the category in either popularity or in the depth with which they addressed the mental condition. For example, *The Silence of the Lambs* provides two contrasting murderers creating a useful comparison in a single work.[17] In *The Dark Knight* the Joker functions as an iconic comic book character that speaks overtly about stereotypical fears about insanity making a person evil.[18] There are also popular works that examine the motives and psychology of the characters in question. Similarly, *Rain Man* operates as a cultural lodestone that has introduced many people to autism spectrum disorder.[19] *Fight Club* is an iconic and often quoted work that manipulates the audience with the trope of the unreliable narrator and simultaneously focuses its intense energy, not on a truthful representation of multiple personality disorder, but rather on the social and political issues being espoused.[20] While the films in the chapter addressing *The Soloist* and *Radio* discuss African American characters with differing mental disorders, this combination in filmmaking appears very rarely.[21]

The first chapter of this book examines how both Fincher's 1999 *Fight Club* and Aronofsky's 2010 *Black Swan* present complex lead characters who initially appear reliable but whose delusions gradually generate ambiguity and doubt about the narrators' mental stability.[22] I feature gender theory and argue that the parallel representations of anxiety and subsequent insanity create a context for illustrating the contrasts in Hollywood's gendered constructions of mental disorder of difference. The main characters in the two films, Nina and Jack, demonstrate the consequences of the quest for embodying not just successfully masculine or feminine versions of themselves but perfect embodiments of America's cultural expectations of gender. The two characters' delusions tell very similar stories of societal expectations, feelings of inadequacy, and gender stereotypes. This chapter will also investigate how the exaggerated nature of the characters' mental disorders communicates the emotional relationship between gender stereotypes and people's experience of gender on film.

The second chapter analyzes the representations that two filmmakers feature to vilify people with mental disorders by making them seem both invisible and contagious. Those with antisocial personality disorder, also known as psychopaths or sociopaths, commonly appear in cinema as evil, murderous villains. Their representations become Othered as these figures play into the height of our cultural insecurity around mental illness. While some, like Hannibal Lecter in *The Silence of the Lambs*, are frightening because their mental difference is obfuscated by their class, others such as Buffalo Bill or the Joker from *The Dark Knight* play into the stereotypes of the madman as infectious vectors of their difference.

The third chapter examines cognitive theoretical studies as a mechanism to understanding cinema's representations of people with autism spectrum disorder. *Rain Man* shows a man on the autism spectrum who the film encourages the audience to like but not identify as or engage with. This condescending type of portrayal speaks to Hollywood cinema's historical lack of investment in positively representing non-neurotypical characters. Using Murray Smith's cognitive approach to understanding character identification, or what he calls engagement, I argue that Raymond is not and cannot be an engaging character even if he is a pleasant or likable character. This is not to say that a filmgoer cannot engage with a person with a mental disability or difference, but that there is a level of disability and its representation that cannot, according to Smith's schema, enact the traits necessary for engagement. Also, Hollywood patterns and expectations of storytelling make the representation of a person with a mental disorder or difference difficult to engage with, which is problematic for many reasons. To establish contrast, I go outside Hollywood to an Australian film. *Mary and Max* does represent a character with significant autism spectrum disorder but one who rises to the level of engagement—not just because of his cognitive abilities, but also, and this is essential, the film provides the audience with enough access to the character's point of view and moral impetus to ensure possible if not probable engagement.[23]

The fourth chapter addresses the intersectional complexity of cinematic representations of people of color with a mental disorder, who rarely appear as main characters in film. Two exceptions to this rule include *Radio* and *The Soloist*. The films depict situations where the condescending and often limiting representations of people with disabilities become compounded by the use of a "white savior" character to resolve the narrative. Each of these films, despite being named for the character with a mental disorder, primarily shows the white male figures who "save" the title characters from their current circumstances. These works demonstrate how Hollywood films commonly represent figures that fit into the overlapping representational issues of the "discourse of pity" as outlined by Michael T. Hayes and Rhonda S. Black and also the problem of "white savior" films. Together these overlapping representational issues create condescending depictions that do not celebrate these characters, but rather subject them to Hollywood's cinematic structures of oppression. *Radio* and *The Soloist* serve as useful examples because while *Radio* presents the epitome of sentimental condescension toward Radio, *The Soloist* performs more admirably, if not entirely equitably, the representation of a person of color with a mental disorder in this genre.

The fifth chapter concerns the representation of authoritarian and institutional governmental power and their ability to gaslight, a term which I use here as an act to convince a person to doubt his or her own perceptions. Characters with mental disorders frequently appear on screen as frightening and dangerous. According to an analysis of numerous research studies done including one by Patricia A. Stout, Jorge Villegas, and Nancy A. Jennings, the media typically depicts people they refer to as mentally ill in negative ways:

> While the body of research examining images of mental illness in media is limited, the findings of these studies are consistent. Content analyses indicate that mental illness is consistently misrepresented in media depictions through exaggerations and misinformation. Depictions are inaccurate, both in representing people as violent and dangerous (Wahl 1992; Philo et al. 1994; Diefenbach 1997) and in the nature of the information about the disorders (Wahl 1992, 1995). The two outstanding conclusions of media portrayals of persons with mental illness are that they are associated with violence and that they are dangerous and should be avoided.[24]

However, *12 Monkeys* and *Girl, Interrupted* raise issues of whether the diagnosis of mental disorder is a justifiable act to shield the innocent or a manipulative mechanism constructed by authoritarian institutions.[25] When the audience views the world from the perspective of the diagnosed person, the authority figures become suspicious and menacing. I use Foucault's work in *Discipline and Punish* to address how these characters become physically and emotionally restrained under the guise of the protection and safety of the public; although, since the character's perspectives dictate the spectators' point of view, the films imbue the people who may have a mental disorder with the authority to govern reality.[26] Mental disorder serves as a cinematic gambit to raise epistemological questions of people's access to knowledge, comprehension of the world, and the importance of who controls society's understanding of truth.

Undoubtedly there are many varied representations of people with mental disorders on film, and this book will not begin to address all of the issues of representation inherent in such a complex and multifaceted issue. Addressing everything is not possible or practical, but this book will attempt to relate to these characters respectfully and in ways that demonstrate their perspective and my belief that people with a mental disorder should have more varied, engaging, respectful, and powerful representation in Hollywood cinema.

NOTES

1. Rosemarie Garland Thompson, *Extraordinary Bodies: Figuring Physical Disability in American Culture and Literature* (New York: Columbia University Press, 1997).
2. Thompson, *Extraordinary Bodies*.

3. Jayci Robb and Jeff Stone, "Implicit Bias toward People with Mental Illness: A Systematic Literature Review." *Journal of Rehabilitation* 82, no. 4 (2016): 9. *CINAHL Complete*, EBSCO*host* (accessed April 22, 2018).

4. Ibid., 3.

5. Stephen Harper, *Madness, Power and the Media: Class, Gender and Race in Popular Representations of Mental Distress* (Basingstoke: Palgrave Macmillan, 2009), 30; and Simon Cross, *Mediating Madness: Mental Distress and Cultural Representation* (London: Palgrave Macmillan, 2010).

6. Harper, *Madness, Power and the Media*, 30.

7. Ibid., 86.

8. Stuart Murray, *Representing Autism: Culture, Narrative, Fascination* (Liverpool: Liverpool University Press, 2008).

9. *Fight Club*, dir. David Fincher (1999; Beverly Hills, CA: Fox 2000 Pictures, 2000), DVD.

10. Harper, Ibid.; Cross, *Mediating Madness*; Naomi Kondo, "Mental illness in film." *Psychiatric Rehabilitation Journal* 31, no. 3 (2018): 250–252.

11. Gregory D. Black, *Hollywood Censored: Morality Codes, Catholics, and the Movies* (New York: Cambridge University Press, 1994).

12. Ibid.

13. Kia Afra, "PG-13, Ratings Creep, and the Legacy of Screen Violence: The MPAA Responds to the FTC's 'Marketing Violent Entertainment to Children' (2000–2009)." *Cinema Journal* 55, no. 3 (2016): 46.

14. Simone de Beauvoir, *The Second Sex* (London: Vintage Books, 1991).

15. Moira Gatens, "Power Bodies and Difference," in *Feminist Theory and the Body: A Reader*, ed. Janet Price and Margrit Shildrick (New York: Routledge, 1999), 227–234.

16. *Mozart and the Whale*, dir. Petter Naess (2005; Los Angeles, CA: Millenium Films); *Adam*, dir. Max Mayer (2009; Los Angeles, CA: Fox Searchlight Pictures); and *The Good Doctor* (2017; Culver City, CA: Sony Pictures Television).

17. *The Silence of the Lambs*, dir. Jonathan Demme (1991; Los Angeles, CA: Orion Pictures, 2001), DVD.

18. *The Dark Knight*, dir. Christopher Nolan (2008; Burbank, CA: Warner Brothers, 2012), DVD.

19. Murray, *Representing Autism*, 88.

20. *Fight Club*.

21. *The Soloist*, dir. Joe Wright (2009; Glendale, CA: Universal, 2009), DVD; and *Radio*, dir. Michael Tollin (2003; Santa Monica, CA: Revolution Studios, 2003), DVD.

22. *Black Swan*, dir. Darren Aronofsky (2011; Beverly Hills, CA: Fox Searchlight Pictures, 2011), DVD.

23. *Mary and Max*, dir. Adam Elliot (2010; Melbourne, Australia: Melodrama Pictures, 2010), DVD.

24. Patricia A. Stout, Jorge Villegas, and Nancy A. Jennings, "Images of Mental Illness in the Media: Identifying Gaps in the Research." *Schizophrenia Bulletin* 30, no. 3 (2004): 543–561.

25. *12 Monkeys*, dir. Terry Gilliam (1995; Universal City, CA: Universal Pictures, 2005), DVD; and *Girl, Interrupted*.

26. Michel Foucault, *Discipline and Punish* (New York: Vintage Books, 1995).

ONE

Gender and Reality in *Fight Club* and *Black Swan*

Dissociative identity disorder or what is more commonly known as multiple personality disorder is a frequent gambit in films to construct a single unreliable character who creates narrative conflict. In some films the character with the apparent dissociative identity disorder is the narrator or central consciousness of a film and thus becomes the filter through which the audience comes to understand the world. In these cases, the audience's perceptions typically become warped by the narrator's point of view. Cinema has told stories of these unreliable insane narrators since such early films as the German expressionist work *The Cabinet of Dr. Caligari*. Both David Fincher's 1999 *Fight Club* and Darren Aronofsky's 2010 *Black Swan* contain these unreliable narrators who skew the audience's ability to reliably comprehend the world presented to them. These altered perceptions allow the audience to become embedded in the anxiety and tension created through the characters' confusion about what constitutes their reality and in these films their extreme relationships to conventional gender expectations. Both main characters' psyches become divided as the characters struggle to become the idealized gendered versions of themselves. They seek to become more "perfect" embodiments of masculinity or femininity, therefore illustrating the unrealistic and sometimes paradoxical expectations of American gender performance in a capitalistic society.

The desire of the main characters in *Fight Club* and *Black Swan* to perform a perfect version of their gender arises from a culture that normalizes and incentivizes firm gendered roles. Neither character appears to overtly question their gender identity in a way that would imply either is a transgendered person, but both feel insecure about the adequacy of their gender performance. Judith Butler's theory of gender is that gender is performative and thus behavior and identity arise from cultural and social expectations rather than being derived inherently from a person's sex. She further asserts in *Undoing Gender*, "To say, however, that gender is performative is not simply to insist on a right to produce a pleasurable and subversive spectacle but to allegorize the spectacular and consequential ways in which reality is both reproduced and contested."[1] Because of their mental disorder, the lead characters in each movie become subsumed under the pressures to perform more perfectly their respective genders. They dislike their current selves at the beginning of these films and seek recognition through more "perfect" gender performance. Judith Butler discusses this connection between identity and gender: "I have tried to argue that our very sense of personhood is linked to the desire for recognition, and that the desire places us outside ourselves, in a realm of social norms that we do not fully choose but that provides the horizon and the resources for any sense of choice that we have."[2] She was specifically addressing concerns of transgendered people who do not conform to their biological sex, but even the gender-conforming Jack and Nina question their own personhood through their feelings of inadequacy about their gender performance. They desire "recognition" from the opposite sex, family, and others to validate them, and these outside cultural sources of validation create paradoxical, dangerous, and harmful demands.

Butler's description of being "outside ourselves"[3] and its connections to our perception of reality speak to the ways that both *Fight Club* and *Black Swan* subvert our expectations of reality. The films undermine the audiences' certainty about what constitutes reality and what is a delusion. This warping of reality appears in other works such as *Shutter Island, Memento, A Beautiful Mind, The Cabinet of Dr. Caligari,* and *Sucker Punch*.[4] Each work encourages the audience to question the reality of what appears before them and whether it has become warped by the perceptions of the narrator. They perhaps also raise the issue of how much of all of our perceptions have been warped by our own point of view and societal expectations.

Fight Club is an exploration of the expectations of masculinity and its relationship to modern contemporary consumerism. The film's unnamed narrator, referred to as Jack in the script and played by Edward Norton, struggles to find his place and identity amid cultural expectations of male behavior, obeisance, and conformity. Numerous academics have documented *Fight Club*'s narrative investment in the insecurities of modern masculinity, including but not limited to consumerism. For example, Lynn M. Ta's article on masculinity in *Fight Club* describes the "portrayal of late capitalism's obsessive push for profits and excessive consumerism, and, more importantly, the latter's damaging effects on an American masculinity gone soft."[5] Jack has a tidy apartment filled with expensive mass-produced furniture, a white-collar job, and no apparent personal relationships. An early scene in the film depicts Jack pacing in his stylish black-and-white apartment as he orders new furniture from a magazine. As he discusses his furniture, he clearly places great emphasis on its importance to him and its corollary monetary value. In an overt critique of consumerism, the prices and catalog descriptions of his furniture appear on-screen as he walks past them. This visual text illustrates not just the titles and names of his furniture but what he paid for each piece. This identifies its value and also connects it to his self-worth, as he has established his value through the material things that surround him. Jack asks himself "what kind of dining set defines me as a person."[6] This transparently shallow lifestyle presents the problematic choices and values that Jack begins rebelling against as he finds his new self-worth in an extremist mode of masculinity.

Figure 1.1. The prices and brands of Jack's furniture appear superimposed over the apartment as if it were in a catalog. David Fincher's 1999 *Fight Club*.

At the beginning of the film, Jack's desire for more expensive and sophisticated furniture and his appreciation for the cost, location, and style of apartment demonstrate his acceptance of these capitalistic markers of success. Yet it becomes clear that he cannot find happiness in this consumerist culture as he could always find better lamps to purchase and more expensive apartments to own. When speaking to the police about the explosion of his apartment, he says, "The condo was my life, okay. I loved every stick of furniture in that place. That was not just a bunch of stuff that got destroyed. That was me."[7] The motivation to buy new things is perpetual and ultimately unrewarding. This investment in these aesthetic, domestic priorities becomes feminine for Jack and according to the film prevents his feeling like he can reach his ultimate masculine fulfillment. However, the film's version of masculine fulfillment occurs when Jack blows up buildings and has aggressive sex with his girlfriend, implying that violence solves his feminization. While the consumerism tells him to value the objects in his home, the masculine ideal the film celebrates conflicts with this notion. This ideal asserts that he should live outside, unconcerned with the domestic space and enjoying physical pain. Henry Giroux overtly criticizes what he claims is the film's blaming of femininity for masculine consumerism and ultimately the character's self-hatred:

> Durden rails against both consumer society and the ongoing feminization of men, both of which contribute to men's feelings of disenfranchisement. He tells Jack early on in the film that men have lost their manhood because they are a generation raised by women and because men have become increasingly defined within the spheres of consumerism and domestication that in our patriarchal, bourgeois society have been stereotypically characterized as the realm of the feminine."[8]

The film illustrates Jack's unhappiness by showing the audience his unfulfilling investment in objects and wealth. The job and the possessions establish a façade of respectability and culturally acceptable success that Jack always wants more of, yet never feels fulfilled by. A Marxist theoretical critique of consumerism including the consequences of capitalism, its lack of concern for the worker, and the unfulfilling dehumanization of modern labor quickly emerges in the film. These characteristics of his life come to represent a modern feminized and sanitized version of the ideal masculinity that the narrator originally desires. This film lambasts modern urbanized masculinity and also Jack for accepting this less violent and less aggressive manifestation of manhood as acceptable and desirable. The film's ultimate rebellion against all things feminine creates an extremely violent and almost comical manifestation of this radical masculinity in Jack's alter ego, Tyler Durden, played by Brad Pitt.

Furthering the capitalist critique, Jack's job as a product-recall specialist at an unnamed car company continues the representation of the seemingly evil consumer culture and its dehumanizing faults. For Jack's unnamed corporation, he assesses the monetary value of recalling a car. According to the narrator, the car company does not determine whether a car should be recalled because of possible dangers to human life, but rather because of the financial consequences of a recall. If the financial cost of hurting people exceeds the financial cost of a recall, then the company recalls a car, but not before. This very financial assessment embodies the Marxist theoretical critique of capitalism's valuing money over and in lieu of human life. His job dehumanizes the customers of the company by reducing people to their monetary value in a lawsuit, and this work subsequently demoralizes Jack. This depression cracks Jack's superficial facade and ostensibly creates his mental instability. His terrible job and the time he spent enduring his seemingly inadequately masculine life leads to his mental breakdown and ultimately his alter ego.

As the film establishes Jack as a cog in the machine of capitalism, it also establishes his societal and emotional representation as a boy rather than a man. When Jack first meets Tyler Durden, he responds to a question about the airplane with "I'm not sure I'm the man for that." While not overtly stating that he is not "a man," it raises the issue of his insecurities and literally his being "the man." Later in the film, he very explicitly states that "I'm a thirty-year-old boy." Ta argues that "In the case of *Fight Club*, [the narrator]'s melancholic sadomasochism is the product of what he perceives to be the feminization of late capitalism; as a corporate drone, he feels victimized by a culture that has stolen his manhood."[9] In his demasculinized state and seemingly as a result of his inability to mature, he develops a dissociative disorder that the film embodies in the form of the hypermasculine violent and sexual alter ego Tyler Durden. If Jack is not "the man for that . . ." then clearly Tyler is. This dissociative identity disorder allows the character to reveal the binary and contradictory expectations about masculinity that commonly appear in film. Jack embodies the sensitive responsible man while also becoming the dangerous aggressor. Tyler becomes all of the kinds of masculinity that Jack wants but cannot become, because the expectations of civility in the urbanized feminized world hold Jack in check. Jack cannot behave in those radically uncivilized ways, but Tyler can, and the dissociative disorder allows him to become his imagined masculine fantasy. *Black Swan* similarly addresses contradictory cultural expectations of gender.

Dissociative identity disorder (DID) is a cinematic gambit that creates the conflict in the film. The *DSM-5* characterizes DID as "by two or more distinct personality states . . . The disruption in identity involves marked discontinuity in sense of self and sense of agency, accompanied by related alterations in affect, behavior, consciousness, memory, perception, cognition, and/or sensor-motor functioning."[10] DID also involves "Recurrent gaps in the recall of everyday events, important personal information, and/traumatic events that are inconsistent with ordinary forgetting."[11] The cinematic representation of this disorder appears as two different actors perform the different manifestations of Jack's personality. This allows the audience to experience Jack's perspective of his illness, without comprehending until the character does, that he and Tyler are both parts of his own psyche. Other films like *A Beautiful Mind* and *Shutter Island* similarly engage in these approaches that, at least for a time, avoid revealing to the audience that the narrator and thus the audience's perspective might be different from what we might otherwise consider reality. Jack experiences gaps in time when the Jack personality does not inhabit the same place as the Tyler personality. This divide in appearance also presents the idealized embodiment of physical masculinity for Jack, who would like to look like the square-jawed and muscular Brad Pitt. The anxieties and tensions about the "perfect" masculinity drive *Fight Club*; and on the flipside of that coin, *Black Swan* addresses the consequences of the drive for "ideal" femininity.

In a feminized reflection of Jack's inadequacies, Natalie Portman's character, Nina Sayers, receives a promotion to become the prima ballerina in *Black Swan*. This boon occurs when her predecessor ages out of the job of the young ingénue of classical ballet. The director has just fired Beth Macintyre, played by Winona Ryder, because of slowing ticket sales and, according to the other characters' comments, her advancing age. The problem of aging becomes clear to the audience as another dancer in the company asserts that in order to increase ticket sales, the ballet needs to "try someone new . . . like someone who is not approaching menopause."[12] Despite Macintyre's apparent age seeming closer to thirty-five than fifty, these comments clearly indicate through tone and context that she has become too old to embody ballet's ideal of the young virginal lead. Macintyre's situation appears as an opportunity and a cautionary tale for the emerging and insecure Nina. The problematic issues of ageism appear reflected in the sexism seen in visual mediums like movies, television, and ballet. Female lead performers and actors appear almost exclusively young, thin, and beautiful. Nina's value as a female performer comes in part from her sex appeal. Nina's desire to embody this perfect young female performer becomes the crux of her psychological problems. She faces the conflicting expectations of innocence and sexuality within the idealized "perfect" ballerina and woman.

While much less overt than *Fight Club,* the ways that Nina's self-worth arises from her labor and her work's value echo Marxist concerns of valuing the worker. Nina's value as a dancer is a large portion of her anxieties. She, as a person, is not a valued part of the ballet company as much as her ability to appeal sexually to the audience and perform the narrative in a pleasing way. Her value becomes what she can produce, rather than who she is.

The older ballerina Macintyre explicitly reinforces the conflict between seeming virginal and sexual as she asserts that the director called Nina a "frigid little girl."[13] This apparent insult implies youth and innocence but ironically expresses neither as positive attributes. In a revealing contradiction, Macintyre immediately turns around and accuses Nina of sleeping with the director and being a "fucking whore." Nina responds that "not everyone does that," which Macintyre takes as an accusation about her own behavior with the director. As much as Macintyre's age disqualifies her from representing the young, virginal, feminine ideal, her insult attempts to disqualify Nina as an asexual girl, then contrastingly as an overly sexual "whore." Nina's subsequent struggle illustrates her fears about being a "whore" or "frigid." Unfortunately, the only road for Nina to become perfect is for her to be both sexual and innocent while being neither the "whore" nor "frigid." This impossible paradox leads to her delusions and psychosis.

More evidence of this fear of being a "whore" occurs in a scene that follows Macintyre's accusations. Nina exits a bathroom stall to read the word "whore" written on a bathroom mirror, yet the word appears in the same red lipstick that Nina recently stole from Macintyre. The scene implies that Nina wrote the accusation herself and feels guilty for something she has done or perhaps something that she wants to do. Her anxiety at seeing the word she wrote herself indicates the beginnings of her disassociation. The film operates from Nina's perspective like *A Beautiful Mind* or *Shutter Island* in the ways that it creates discomfort and anxiety as an early clue to a larger psychological mystery. The audience comes to solve the mystery along with the narrator. She has begun to lose time, and she unconsciously fears the implications of Macintyre's accusation, despite her seemingly virginal status.

Another stressor for Nina and a symptom of her psychological trouble manifests through an eating disorder that later becomes an extreme body dysmorphic disorder (BDD), where she imagines herself becoming the swan. BDD has close diagnostic and psychological ties to disorders like anorexia and bulimia.[14] Nina's mother and the ballet culture place Nina under extreme pressure to maintain the adolescently feminine "ideal" body for ballet. Nina looks very skinny throughout the film, with collar bones visible and a petite frame. The film illustrates her issues with food through her grapefruit and poached egg breakfast. The audience hears Nina admire the slight breakfast, and the camera presents it to the audience to ensure our attention. This emphasis raises doubt about the adequacy of such a small meal for a professional athlete like a ballet dancer. This calorie restriction demonstrates for the audience the extreme rigor of her routine and implies a dangerous relationship with her body image.

Figure 1.2. Nina's scant breakfast of half a grapefruit and one poached egg. Darren Aronofsky's 2011 *Black Swan*.

This food issue appears again later when her mother, Erica Sayers as played by Barbara Hershey, purchases a celebratory cake. Upon receiving the part of the swan in *Swan Lake*, Nina's mother buys a large vanilla cake with strawberry filling. Because of the mother's awareness of Nina's food restrictions, the choice to buy a cake appears like a manipulative attempt to either sabotage her success or demonstrate her continued control of Nina. After Nina's initial refusal to eat much, her mother grabs the cake and moves toward the garbage to throw it all away as if insulted.

Her use of guilt forces Nina to eat some of the cake, which demonstrates her mother's control and manipulation. Nina even eats the initial bite of icing off of her mother's finger. This awkward childish closeness feels inappropriate for an adult child and her mother. Much like with Jack, Nina's inability to behave fully as an adult becomes part of her problem. As the only father figure in the film, the ballet director asks her to be both the virgin and the whore simultaneously, her childish need to please him tears her apart.

Along with the food restrictions, which imply a level of anorexia, a later scene shows Nina throwing up in the bathroom either through stress or as evidence of bulimia. While grapefruit does not necessarily indicate anorexia, the explicit imagery of the small portions of an already skinny athlete and later images of her throwing up reinforce the implication of an unhealthy relationship with food. Anorexia manifests as eating too few calories, and the *DSM-5* describes it as similar to obsessive-compulsive disorders.[15] This is one of several signs that Nina lacks mental and emotional stability, and her attempt at becoming the ideal woman has become an obsession. Her desire for perfection drives her mad. She even states in the film, "I want to be perfect."[16] These concerns do not stand alone as Nina's primary problem, but rather as symptoms of the body dysmorphic disorder that develops by the end of the film.

Throughout the film, the characters around her reinforce Nina's insecurities about her body and her natural expressive dance. Nina fights for the lead part while listening to comments from the director, played by Vincent Cassel, that despite her precise "perfect" form, she may not get the part because she cannot "lose herself" and "let go."[17] Her profession demands exacting control and precision in training, eating, and movements, and suddenly the director informs her that her dancing feels too controlled and exacting. The director tells her, to dance by telling her "Not so controlled . . . Seduce us. . . ."[18] For him, she embodies the "virginal innocent" white swan. However, he does not initially believe she can also embody the emotive and passionate black swan. She has labored her entire life to become the perfect feminine ideal ballerina, and now the director tells her that she tries too hard and that it should come naturally. Nina internalizes the criticism; and immediately Mila Kunis's character, Lily, enters the scene. Lily promptly becomes her rival, sexual role model, and briefly her imagined sexual partner.

Lily exemplifies a figure for whom dancing comes "naturally." The film indicates that this serves as the preferred state, which Nina admires and desires for herself. Lily does not appear tense in the way that Nina does, and she is worldly and reckless in her approach to dating and drugs. She takes Nina to the bar and flirts successfully with men while Nina struggles. Lily personifies the sexuality that Nina cannot embody in her childlike ignorance. Nina desires to be sexual to fulfill the expectations of her director, but she also fears sexuality as noted by her own accusatory writing on the mirror calling herself a whore. Her anxieties about becoming too sexualized can be understood as tension about virginity and purity that operates as a central conceit of the fundamentally Puritan American culture. This fear of sexual promiscuity has informed the representations of sexualized women in many films and their resultant punishment or death.

The film continues to depict Nina's infantilization through her relationship with her domineering and manipulative mother and her childish and unlockable bedroom. Their first conversation shows her mother's manipulation. Nina states that the director "promised to feature me more."[19] Her mother replies in a backhanded compliment, "Well, he certainly should. You've been there long enough, and you're the most dedicated dancer in the company."[20] She hints at Nina's age as a ballerina who may be moving past her prime, and at the same time, she soothes her with a comment about her effort. The room remains filled with the detritus of Nina's youth including stuffed animals, music boxes, and a ruffled pink duvet. The childish items illustrate her general immaturity and her particular need for reassurance and stability. The bedroom door does not even initially have a lock, which reinforces her innocence and an absence of boundaries between Nina and her mother. Only subsequent to a scene where her mother almost catches her masturbating does Nina find a way to secure her door. Her exploration of her sexuality and the undermining of her ideal virginal innocence begin to initiate the fracturing of Nina's identity. The classically misogynistic Hollywood film does not usually depict a woman complicated enough to simultaneously embody both the white swan and the black swan. In "Debating Black Swan: Gender and Horror," Amber Jacobs "argues that Black Swan represents 'another tired binary mapping the limited terrain of femininity under patriarchy: the white/black, virgin/whore split which the film makes no attempt to disrupt.'"[21] Nina's lack of maturity forces this split between the virgin and the whore, and Hollywood cinema's classically oversimplistic depiction of women does not provide much opportunity for Nina or any woman to exist as both good and sexual.

Along with being part of classic Hollywood's limiting of female characters, *Black Swan* also retells a fairy tale that literally depicts a good woman and a bad woman as white and black. The film parallels two characters from the original ballet of *Swan Lake*. The white swan represents the sweet, innocent, virginal object of the prince's affection. The daughter of an evil sorcerer impersonates the white swan and uses her feminine wiles to attract the prince and doom the white swan to the sorcerer's curse. This fairy tale, like many, depicts women in the simplistic terms of the virgin or the whore. As a classic Hollywood film, *Black Swan* similarly follows a long tradition of objectified female characters established for the pleasure of the male gaze and tied to the formulaic options for a character's portrayal.

In both *Black Swan* and *Fight Club*, the pointedly gendered expressions of the characters' insecurities drive Jack and Nina insane. Their delusions arise as they face their inability to conform to idealized notions of either femininity or masculinity. This places enormous narrative value on gender conformity because failure to become properly feminine or masculine leads to disaster and trauma. The audience sees this further played out through the symptoms and damage created by their insanity. The most prominent narrative symptom appears as imaginary companions or alter egos who help them realize wish fulfillment and establish emotional connections with romantic interests.

The film *Sucker Punch* works along these same lines, as the main character who is only known as Babydoll (Emily Browning) fights to escape a mental institution. In some of the ways that *Fight Club* and *Black Swan* construct unreal worlds around the hopes and ambitions of their central figures, Babydoll imagines her way out of the place she finds herself in. The hyperfeminized Babydoll is envisioned as a strong, if very sexualized, figure that tries to escape an unjust lobotomy. Most of the film exists in her imaginary world, and the audience's understanding of reality reflects the confused narrator. Babydoll like Nina finds herself surrounded by controlling manipulative men who force her to embrace gender conformity.

In *Fight Club* the alter ego Tyler becomes Jack's version of the cinematic masculine ideal. Tyler appears as an assertive, aggressive rebel whose sexual prowess pleases women and whose physical endurance proves his strength and dominance. Tyler does everything that Jack wishes he could do but cannot because of fear, decency, and anxiety. Tyler becomes Jack's sexual surrogate as he sleeps with the love interest Marla, played by Helena Bonham Carter. Tyler's fearlessness also helps him initiate the first fight that ultimately results in the creation of the fight club. Tyler's aggressive nature allows him to create his organizations and then lead the members of Fight Club and Project Mayhem. Under Tyler's tutelage, these recruits ultimately destroy the credit card companies that they see as the root of the materialistic, capitalistic, and feminine problems in the world. The film aligns materialism with femininity, framing it as undesirable and emasculating.

Even Tyler's home, a traditionally feminine and materialistic space, eschews all of the traditional femininity of a home. The old rickety house sits in a commercial district avoiding neighbors or society. Social and familial interactions imply a more female environment in opposition to, for example, a hypermasculine stoic cowboy from a Hollywood western. The house's location and isolation make it an antisocial, dangerous, and masculine space. The house does not appear safe, comfortable, or domestic in the ways that Jack's previous apartment did. The house virtually leaves the characters outside by leaking and having unreliable or no electricity. While being a place they can reside, it avoids the materialistic trappings. The house's aesthetic does not function as a welcoming feminine space but a site of resistance. They live as close to the wild West as possible while residing in downtown Los Angeles.

Like Tyler, Nina's alter ego allows her to "let go" and "lose yourself" and dance as both the white swan and the black swan, but she also provides Nina with love.[22] Her dissociative identity disorder constructs the delusion of a friend/lover relationship and gives her the feeling of the adult validation that she has sought. Because this validation comes from within, it should be positive, but because of the nature of her delusions, it quickly becomes destructive.

The audience first sees the separation between Nina and herself in mirrors. The audience frequently sees Nina's reflection in mirrors putting on makeup, warming up, practicing, and in restrooms. She can also be seen reflected in glass on the subway, and in the remarkably similar appearance of Lily. While on the train, Nina sees Lily; the audience sees a match-on-action between Lily and Nina, giving the confusing impression that they are the same person. This subtle ploy in the cinematography makes the audience unsure of what they saw and what they understand, which foreshadows Nina's mental decay and the audience's unreliable perception of that.

The cinematography throughout the film shows Nina again and again as divided from herself and split between how we see her and how she sees herself. Her reflections in mirrors and ultimately in her mother's paintings begin moving independently of Nina. This feeds on her insecurity and indicates to the audience that they should doubt Nina and her unstable perceptions. As Aronofsky aligned the narrative with Nina's perspective, her delusions become the audience's. When she forgets that she wrote "whore" on the mirror, the audience does not see the original act. When Nina sees her image in mirrors move independently of her, the audience sees them as well. During several points in the film, the audience sees Nina in front of a mirror while dancing. In Gabrielle O'Brien's article "Mirror, Mirror: Fractured Female Identity in Black Swan," she describes how "Mirrors routinely dominate the mise en scène, suggesting that Nina's fragile self-identity is entirely contained and defined by external 'surface' reflections; she is effectively reduced to what she sees staring back at her in the mirror."[23] During Nina's decline, the mirrored image makes another rotation before stopping. The mirror self also scratches the uncomfortable spot on Nina's back, startling Nina. As the audience understands that Nina has been picking at her back largely unconsciously, to have the conscious self see the unconscious self act feels starkly uncomfortable.

Perhaps the most disturbing of the independently moving images of Nina appears through her mother's paintings. Nina goes into her mother's room to see the many painted versions of her own face. As warped abstractions of Nina, as composed by her mother's hand, they show her incomplete face over and over. They imply both how much Nina's mother has shaped her and also how incomplete Nina feels as a person. She has not matured fully and remains unfinished. In one of the final scenes of the film, these paintings come alive and cry back at Nina, "Sweet girl" and "It's my turn."[24] Her mother's words emerge from her mother's distorted images of Nina. She does not have a stable understanding of herself, so the understandings of others formulate her identity and ultimately her desire for perfection. The film's first-person structure and unreliable narrator destabilize the reality presented in the narrative.

Figure 1.3. Nina's mother's studio includes numerous paintings of Nina with various tortured expressions. Darren Aronofsky's 2011 *Black Swan*.

As this destabilized viewpoint comes in painted images, we might conclude that our understandings of ourselves are not fixed but filtered through others and others' representations. In the film *Memento*, the lead character has lost his short-term memory and so tattoos information on himself and gives himself clues to understand his past. However, the information that he gives himself does not always match reality. The audience learns this as the narrative progresses in largely reverse order. He is subject to the lies he tells himself about how the world is. In much the same way, Nina has internalized the social and cultural expectations of ideal womanhood.

The director of *Black Swan*, Aronofsky, teases Nina with the possibility of a solution to her problems of perfection. The ideal perfect woman to the male director, Thomas Leroy, embodies both the white and the black swan; she is simultaneously both innocent and sexual. Nina's struggle with that conflict brings her to Lily, who initially appears open and accepting of Nina's current self. This potential lesbian relationship provides Nina with a level of acceptance that she does not receive from her director or her mother. Nina seeks external validation and feeds on Lily's compliments. This initial friendship becomes corrupted in Nina's fragile mind, and she ultimately imagines their sexual encounter. The audience sees their relationship as if it actually happened, and the film does not provide much immediate cause to question their encounter. Only when Lily denies their encounter does the audience strongly doubt that it happened outside Nina's mind. Lily's denial of Nina becomes the breaking point where Nina and the audience realize the full extent of her delusions.

In "In Debating Black Swan: Gender and Horror," Mark Fisher argues for the film's disruption of the normative gaze and claims, "Throughout most of the film, Nina will not allow herself to be constituted as a sexual object, even for herself."[25] However, that would imply a pride or maturity that led her to remain virginal. Her overall lack of maturity, willingness to masturbate when instructed by her boss, and the sexual wish fulfillment would all imply that she does not desire to remain innocent. Nina's naiveté implies that her innocence and ignorance operate as by-products of her sheltered childhood and mental fragility. She would like to become the sexy, natural, black swan figure, but she does not appear to know how throughout most of the film. She has spent her time and energy in life learning the perfection of the white swan and being isolated from the sexuality of its darker counterpart. She struggles because she has embodied one type of femininity, but for this role, the director asks her to simultaneously fit two separate disparate ideals.

Ultimately, even Nina's imaginary friend seems to betray her, and she attempts to stab Lily, but in her delusion she has actually stabbed herself. Only at this moment of penetrating her own skin and embodying the male and female does she fulfill the role of the "perfect" ballet performance. Of course, she cannot live in this split binary and ultimately psychotic "perfect" state. This moment represents the character's and more generally women's failure to "have it all," especially since the "all" that Nina seeks includes being simultaneously sexual and virginal, exact and natural, controlled and free.

Another similarity between the structures of *Black Swan* and *Fight Club* appears as Nina and Jack's imaginary counterparts become their sexual surrogates, each serving as a kind of masturbatory bridge to adult sexual validation. In their respective prepubescent states, they struggle to be sexual or have sex, but their uninhibited alter egos allow them to connect sexually with other people, or at least imaginary other people. The consequences of these sexual encounters create complications for both narratives.

For Nina, the real Lily's denial and their awkward postcoital encounter serve as part of the precipitating events leading to her fall. Her realization of revelatory sex that allowed her to rebel against her mother's oppressive attachment was crushed when she realized it was all in her head. Her disappointment spurred her continued rebellion and the audience's awareness of her delusions. For Jack, the consequences were less fatal. Despite the fights and angst created by his/Tyler's sexual relationship with Marla, the film ends in his holding hands with Marla in an unsettling and hopeful moment while they watch the credit card company buildings explode. In all of the mayhem of Jack's multiple personalities and mental decline, Jack finds confidence in his original self and fights back against the extreme Tyler. By fighting and opposing his extreme alter ego, it helps Jack feel better and become stronger, just as his masochistic fighting club asserts it will. The film establishes fighting as the solution to men's problems. Ultimately Jack overcomes his alter ego, while Nina dies at the height of her success, because the loss of innocence is the marker of Jack's success as a man but not for Nina as a woman.

Figure 1.4. Jack and Marla romantically hold hands and look at each other in the final scene of the film. David Fincher's 1999 *Fight Club*.

As with the delusions of their narrators' counterparts, both films represent self-injury and masochism developing from their inadequacies. In *Fight Club*, even while the audience believes that Tyler Durden and Jack fight other people, the action begins when Jack actually hits himself in the parking lot of a bar. Tyler asks Jack to hit him. He does not begin by hitting another man but by wanting to be hit. They create the fight clubs not only as places to hit other men, but especially as places to experience being hit. The characters relish the pain as a means of feeling "alive" and even calling the masochist acts "premature enlightenment," relating it to "premature ejaculation." They celebrate pain as a means to access emotions or a higher consciousness. In the ultimate demonstration of suffering and self-inflicted pain, Jack proves his ultimate machismo when he suffers a burn given by Tyler. The film implies Jack becomes a better and wiser man for having experienced the pain.

Ironically Nina's long-term self-discipline, physical endurance, and suffering fit beautifully the masculine ideal presented in *Fight Club*. Nina's shown doing grueling spins over and over in an effort to achieve the perfection that she seeks. She works incredibly hard to achieve her goals, and her discipline remains evident throughout the film. The film pauses at several points to focus on Nina's feet after she cracks a toenail and to show her blisters. Her psychological drama appears as she picks at cuticles and scratches at her back. Her self-mutilation shows her anxiety and the pressure that she puts on herself. She suffers and endures for what she wants. The pain that Tyler puts Jack through is just momentary angst in the face of Nina's years of pain for her art. In her effort to become the perfect woman, she endures the suffering of the perfect man.

Nina suffers most of her self-inflicted injuries more quietly and shamefully than Jack. Her self-destructive tendencies appear to fall into two general categories: culturally accepted damage in the extreme athletic training and anorexia/ bulimia, and culturally unacceptable damage in the scratching and picking at her skin. Throughout the film, the scratching of her back and the picking at her cuticles appear as a dirty little secret that must be covered up under shawls and generally concealed from others. This picking behavior also appears to be a precursor to her later extreme physical delusions. According to the *DSM-5*, body dysmorphic disorder includes several criteria that fit Nina's perceptions. One of these criteria involves picking: "At some point . . . the individual has performed repetitive behaviors (e.g., mirror checking, excessive grooming, skin picking, reassurance seeking) . . . The preoccupation causes clinically significant distress or impairment in social, occupational, or other important areas of functioning."[26] Nina hurts herself, much like Jack in *Fight Club*, yet without the triumphantly masculine affirmation seen in the other film. Because the scratches and injuries mar her physical beauty in visible ways, she hides it, in contrast with the *Fight Club* characters who wear their bruises and scars with pride. The men do not prioritize their physical beauty as their physical prowess, and the way they demonstrate their aggression serves their active and external purposes. Nina feels shame for her scratching because as much as her calorie restrictions, injured feet, and grueling practice also injure her body, they do not injure her embodiment of this feminine ideal. These injuries conform to the conventions of beauty or dance in ways that reaffirm her femininity, while the scratching conflicts with it, making it singularly shameful. In contrast, Jack's self-injury brings triumphant and masculine affirmations celebrating his bravery and endurance.

The climaxes of these two films continue to follow through with depictions of self-injury, and the results reaffirm societal expectations of gender in largely problematic ways. The conventions of Hollywood cinema commonly force dangerous, sexual, or complex women into untenable positions that result in their death. As with the femme fatale, Hollywood does not typically celebrate the powerful woman, and Nina in her moment of perfection becomes too masculine and powerful as she penetrates herself with the broken glass. She cannot, therefore, survive the cinematic and fairy-tale imperative to destroy the now black swan or ultimately the powerful sexual woman. In these two films, the depictions coalesce and reward the masculine outward societal expressions of pain;

in contrast, the more feminine inward suffering and self-mutilation result in death.

In contrast to Nina's internal self-destructive behavior, Jack's violence extends outward and attacks the economic infrastructure that he sees as the cause of his suffering. Unlike Nina, he does not blame himself but society for infantilizing him. He also mentions his own immaturity but places the blame on his absent father and cultural expectations. The external impersonal violence that erupts is grounded in the masculine representation of rage as seen in numerous Hollywood films. Man versus the government, man versus injustice, man versus capitalism, and man versus the world are all common film tropes. In Jack's final confrontation with Tyler, Jack shoots himself to destroy his alter ego, Tyler, but Jack still survives. In contrast, Nina stabs her alter ego but actually stabs herself and dies. Whereas Tyler's departure leaves Jack the chance to move on, cinema allows no forgiveness or opportunity for Nina to survive her final self-mutilation.

Leading up to and precipitating her self-mutilation, Nina experiences moments of extreme body dysmorphic disorder, which is understood as seeing oneself dramatically differently than one actually is. The *DSM-5* states that people with BDD have a "Preoccupation with one or more perceived defects or flaws in physical appearance that are not observable or appear slight to others."[27] While self-perception can be an amorphous thing, persons with BDD will see themselves as fat even if they are severely malnourished. They will often become fixated on perceived problems with their physical self. Nina does not see herself as she is, but she and the film audience see her literally become the black swan and "let go" of her physical and sane self. During her last dance, her legs buckle backward in supremely uncomfortable moments. She physically becomes both the character of the black swan and the bird. In these moments she becomes quite literally the swan that ultimately leads to her final transformation and release. She cannot be herself in her physical state, but she must become something more to be "perfect." She says after stabbing herself with one of the many mirrors in the film, "I felt it. It was perfect." Her search for perfection becomes self-destructive, and she cannot survive her ultimate perfection.

In *Fight Club*, Tyler states, "Self-improvement is masturbation. Now self-destruction . . ." He leaves the thought trailing off but clearly implies that self-destruction is like sex rather than like masturbation. In these films, destruction, like sex, is "pregnant" with possibility. Self-destruction can become productive in a way that inspires creativity or rebellion, which the narrative celebrates. For Nina the notion of a productive self-destruction appears ironically true. She does become the perfect swan, but she pays the ultimate price. She must destroy herself in order to achieve perfection.

In a typical Hollywood movie, or perhaps more specifically a traditional patriarchal puritan approach, because she is a woman, she cannot be forgiven or redeemed after her sexual transgressions. As film has often shown, a woman gets to represent the virgin or the whore, the damsel or the stepmother, and once she sins, the film cannot rehabilitate her. Nina must suffer the consequences of her actions. She dies, where Jack, despite having shot himself, gets to live happily ever after. The pain of these characters' inability to fulfill their idealized notions of gender drives them insane. This strongly reaffirms the importance of meeting expectations of gender conformity and the consequences of failing.

The construction of these two texts as confusing reality for the audience can be understood as drawing attention to particular points of view not necessarily reflective of reality. As in the way that *Sucker Punch* constructs multiple planes of reality and the delusions serve to romanticize the pain and suffering of the protagonist, *Fight Club* and *Black Swan* create worlds or experiences that do not reflect reality. However, if all of our experience of reality is always filtered, then reality is not fixed. If our understanding of the world is positional, then certainly concepts such as gender need not be fixed as absolutes. Gender and these characters' experience of it are positional and different in ways that inform their own reality in varied ways. Each of these films highlights the limitations and positionality of each viewpoint.

NOTES

1. Judith Butler, *Undoing Gender* (New York: Routledge, 2004), 30.
2. Ibid., 33.
3. Ibid.
4. *Shutter Island, Memento, A Beautiful Mind, The Cabinet of Dr. Caligari,* and *Sucker Punch.*
5. Lynn M. Ta, "Hurt so Good: Fight Club, Masculine Violence, and the Crisis of Capitalism." *Journal of American Culture,* no. 3 (2006): 265.
6. *Fight Club,* dir. David Fincher (1999; Beverly Hills, CA: Fox 2000 Pictures, 2000), DVD.
7. Ibid.
8. Henry A. Giroux and Imre Szeman, "IKEA Boy and the Politics of Male Bonding: Fight Club, Consumerism, and Violence." *New Art Examiner* 28, no. 4 (2000): 35.
9. *Fight Club.*
10. *Diagnostic and Statistical Manual of Mental Disorders: Fifth Edition*, (Washington DC: American Psychiatric Association, 2013), 292.
11. Ibid.
12. *Black Swan,* dir. Darren Aronofsky (2011; Beverly Hills, CA: Fox Searchlight Pictures, 2011), DVD.
13. Ibid.
14. *DSM-5,* 242.
15. Ibid., 341.
16. *Black Swan.*
17. Ibid.
18. Ibid.

19. Ibid.
20. Ibid.
21. Mark Fisher and Amber Jacobs, "Debating Black Swan: Gender and Horror," *Film Quarterly* 65, no. 1 (2011): 59.
22. *Black Swan*.
23. Gabrielle O'Brien, "Mirror, Mirror: Fractured Female Identity in Black Swan," *Screen Education*, no. 75 (2014): 102.
24. Ibid.
25. Fisher and Jacobs, "Debating Black Swan," 59.
26. *DSM-5*, 242.
27. Ibid.

TWO

Villainizing and Psychopaths in *The Dark Knight* and *The Silence of the Lambs*

Films frequently present people with a mental disorder, especially those with antisocial personality disorder, as violent or dangerous. *No Country for Old Men, Monster, Cape Fear, Psycho, The Talented Mr. Ripley, Dirty Harry, Training Day, Natural Born Killers, A Clockwork Orange, American Psycho*, and *Taxi Driver* include just a few of the films that present such killers. The number of works is extensive and goes beyond film into criminals in numerous television shows including *Law and Order, Criminal Minds, CSI, Dexter,* and *Bosch*.

These representations of people with a mental disorder speak to real cultural anxieties. According to the U.S. Department of Health and Human Services, "The vast majority of people with mental health problems are no more likely to be violent than anyone else. Most people with mental illness are not violent and only 3%–5% of violent acts can be attributed to individuals living with a serious mental illness. In fact, people with severe mental illnesses are over 10 times more likely to be victims of violent crime than the general population."[1] These statistical realities do not reflect the common depictions on television and in film.

If people with a mental disorder do not pose a significant threat, why then do these violent figures appear so dominantly in the collective media? I argue that it is because mental disorder is an invisible and incalculable Other that people fear is somehow contagious. Our cultural and social anxieties about the Other become crystallized in a figure who either cannot be immediately distinguished from normates or who does not conform to familiar social paradigms. This makes the Othering particularly scary, because these Others could be masquerading as normates and "passing" as neurotypical, or they are people who cannot be controlled by typical social expectations. They can then infect normates with their madness.

Frequently the scary Other figure in violent films could be diagnosed as a person with antisocial personality disorder (APD), also often commonly known as a person with psychopathy or sociopathy. The serial killers in *The Dark Knight* and *The Silence of the Lambs*, Hannibal Lecter, Jame Gumb, and the Joker, have many of these diagnostic markers in common. Despite some pop culture implications in shows like *Sherlock,* which imply that these terms mean different things, all three words refer to the same diagnosis in psychiatry. The current *DSM-5* uses the term antisocial personality disorder (APD) and it includes symptoms like "a pervasive pattern of disregard for and violation of the rights of others."[2] This feature of APD demonstrates a person's lack of awareness or consideration for other people and their feelings. This lack of regard for others can also result in a "failure to conform to social norms with respect to lawful behaviors, as indicated by repeatedly performing acts that are grounds for arrest" and "reckless disregard for safety of self or others."[3] When committing these crimes and creating these problems for other people, they also demonstrate a "lack of remorse, as indicated by being indifferent to or rationalizing having hurt, mistreated, or stolen from another."[4] These problems are paired with deceitfulness, irritability, and finally aggressiveness.[5] Audiences can identify several of these symptoms in both *The Silence of the Lambs'* serial killers and the Joker in *The Dark Knight*, such as unlawful behavior, deceit, lack of remorse, disregard for others, and aggressiveness.[6] Most serial killers in film can probably be attributed to some level of this diagnosis. While sometimes spree killers or killers who murder numerous people quickly such as school shooters or workplace killers exhibit immediate mental breaks with reality or consequences, serial killers are often depicted as cognizant that their crimes are wrong, attempt to cover them up, and commit them regardless of the moral implications. These characteristics imply a criminal with APD.

These killers appear in numerous films. For example, *No Country for Old Men* depicts a man who murders people without apparent remorse; and like *The Dark Knight*'s Two-Face, Harvey Dent uses a coin flip to determine if he will kill someone.[7] This lack of consideration of the victim's humanity on Anton Chigurh's (Javier Bardem) part places him in this category. Charlize Theron's depiction of Aileen Wuornos in *Monster* similarly depicts a figure who, in the film, knowingly murdered men over a span of time and did so consciously aware of the moral implications of her actions.[8] *Monster,* unlike some of these other films, was based on a true story of an extremely rare female serial killer. Each of these representations is a frightening depiction that seeks to evoke fear of characters with APD. Aileen operates as an exception to many of these films, where the film does attempt to evoke some sympathy for the tragedy that filled her early life experiences, but Chigurh, the Joker, Gumb, and Lecter are constructed in ways that inspire fear, not empathy. This variance may be attributed to her exception as the lone female killer, but it may also occur because the character was based on a recent female serial killer. Wuornos has a known and well-documented tragic history that provides context and explanation for a kind of psychology that many of us find unfathomable.[9]

A Batman film, *The Dark Knight* came out in 2008 as the center film in a trilogy reboot. This iteration of Batman includes Christian Bale performing its title character. This film followed *Batman Begins* (2005) and preceded *The Dark Knight Rises* (2012).[10] All directed by Christopher Nolan, the central film positions Batman in opposition to the Joker as played by Heath Ledger. Batman has hindered much of the criminal underworld since his inception as the Caped Crusader the previous year. The Joker steals from a bank and then allies himself with the remaining criminals in an effort to destroy Batman. The two adversaries play games, alternately the cat and the mouse in their attempts to destroy the other.

The Joker appears as a contemporized comic book villain. In this iteration of the franchise, the Joker wears messy exaggerated clown makeup and a bright purple suit. Unlike some of the earlier iterations of the Joker, Ledger's makeup looks consistently shabby as if he has worn it for so long that it is sweating and rubbing off. Painted mostly white, his red lips are drawn over his mouth and up the sides of his face that oddly obscures and highlights his scars. The scars make him look like he has a perpetual if forced smile. The white of his face appears faded or eroded, especially around the lines in his forehead, giving him a fatigued look. The black around his eyes provides his face a sunken appearance that emphasizes the tired, disordered expression, which has drifted from what one imagines originated as a playful clown face to a wasted crazy mien. The Joker's makeup operates as a mask and reinforces his mental disorder and instability. He paints his mental disorder and difference onto his face. This facade, which helps him appear dangerous, serves the character's purposes as he desires to incite chaos and fear. He becomes the embodiment of visible, recognizable mental disorder, thus symbolizing chaos to frighten film audiences as well his fictional foes. This visible mental disorder seems especially reminiscent of comic books, where his insides match his outsides. Audiences would perhaps like to imagine that mental disorders function as something that one can identify visually. It would be comforting to imagine that one could tell when a person has a mental disorder. The Joker creates a superficial and in some ways a stereotypical way of conceptualizing mental disorder as something measurable and obvious. The stereotypes about mental disorder establish that it affects people in obvious, consistent, and predictable ways. It also happens to Other people, particularly scary villainous people with tragic histories. The Joker plays neatly into those preconceptions.

Figure 2.1. The Joker's makeup looks worn, and it emphasizes the scars around his mouth. Christopher Nolan's 2008 *The Dark Knight*.

The Joker's physical wearing of mental disorder through his makeup relays a superficial understanding of people with a mental disorder, which implies a simplistic kind of emotional confusion. His messy, painted smile in contrast with the darkness around his eyes appears deceptive or disordered. It reads as a visual manipulation of emotion. His scars mean that his smile is incised into his cheeks and permanently forced. The manufactured smile, however, does not clearly reflect his darker underlying expression or sentiments. The makeup smile is misleading and ironic in the ways that mental disorder can encourage actual people to wear a mask or a facade in an effort to evade the stigma of mental disorder. The Joker does not intend to avoid notice; another character describes it as his "war paint." While denying that he has a mental disorder in one scene with a group of mobsters, the Joker clearly revels in manipulating expectations. The Joker's failure to pass as sane makes his disorder more emphatic and plays upon spectator fears of people with mental disorders.

Analogously, Batman operates as a character who also wears a mask and experiences, what the film seems to posit as post-traumatic stress disorder from the loss of his family at a young age. Batman uses his trauma for good rather than evil, which sets him in contrast with the Joker and his narratives of previous trauma. Their disguises inform how they want others to perceive them, and by doing so they physically reflect their own mental disorders.

Part of the makeup overlays the scars around the Joker's mouth. He tells several different stories about how he got his scars. While he specifically discusses his physical scars, the varied versions of the story clearly imply that if they were true, they would also refer to how he became mentally scarred. He tells one story, where he cut himself for a loved one, one story where his father abused him, and he begins to tell a third version before being stopped. These different narratives are self-serving lies the Joker uses to manipulate his victims, but they also highlight the audience's desire to understand the origins of his mental disorder. The audience wants to know what drove him to his current evil behavior. This illustrates the unease of audiences with the vague or seemingly random origins of actual mental disorder. The Joker's stories also show that a person who may have started sane can be driven insane by circumstances out of their control. If one can understand the beginnings of madness, then one can theoretically avoid it, and the Joker's muddled origin story obscures what instigated his insanity. This spreads the frightening notion that anyone similarly could be driven to mental disorder and evil.

Leading other people to insanity or at least insane behavior operates as part of his goal. His insanity feels contagious. The Joker makes Harvey Dent turn evil or mentally unstable, which results in his murdering people based on a literal coin flip. By making people crazy, the Joker plays upon the fear that mental disorder can be contagious.[11] If its beginning cannot be predicted, it cannot be prevented. This leaves the danger of mental disorder as one that cannot be cured, but a random and distinctly terrifying affliction.

One of the Joker's consistent behaviors in the film occurs as he invades people's personal space. The first place this happens is with a mobster who has put a bounty on his life. Just before killing him, the Joker stands very close and holds a knife to his face. The intimacy of the moment feels invasive and deliberately unsettling. Another example of the Joker's invasion of personal space occurs at a political fund-raiser where the Joker breaks in looking for Batman. When the Joker threatens Rachel Dawes (Maggie Gyllenhaal), he clutches at her face and holds her against him. She struggles but does not successfully pull away. The camera rotates around the couple closely as if in mockery of a romantic dance scene. It alternates between closeups and extreme closeups, making the proximity with the Joker's deteriorating makeup disturbing. His invasion of her and the audience's space is a deliberate way of making people uneasy. He stands too close while licking his lips awkwardly and plays up the uncomfortable feeling that he could contaminate Dawes with his mental disorder. The film evokes discomfort by making his mental disorder seem communicable and playing upon the fears of spectators.

Part of the Joker's greatest strength as an unsettling villain happens in the way that he creates random acts of violence. It is reassuring to imagine that violence occurs at a distance, and Others cause it. This distance creates an impression of security. However, the randomness and the lack of reason in the Joker's choices make him a force of nature that keeps people from being able to argue with him or predict his future attacks. Because the characters in the story do not understand him, they cannot easily capture and stop him. Batman's butler, Alfred, tells a story about working in Burma and encountering a warlord who would steal precious jewels and then throw them away. When asked the warlord's motives for his violence and theft, Alfred asserts, "Some men just want to watch the world burn," which implies a scary incurable psychopathy feeding off of people's implicit bias toward those with mental disorder. Robb and Stone in their systematic literature review of mental disorder state, "People with mental illness continue to be a stigmatized group, encountering negative attitudes and discriminatory behaviors from others."[12] The film uses this fear by having other characters refer to the Joker as a "wack job" and "crazy" to reinforce the unpredictable figure.

The Joker is a visual embodiment of violent mental disorder. His characterization as a figure who looks crazy makes him encompass the superficial fears about the classic cinematic psychopathic killer. His outward expression of mental disorder appears inverted in Hannibal Lecter. Lecter operates as a man who for most of the film appears sane. Lecter seems cordial, polite, sophisticated, and he hides his complete lack of regard for others' emotions in his pleasant erudite facade. While the Joker looks crazy and plays with his own unpredictable psychopathy to manipulate his victims and encourage fear, Lecter conceals and obscures his mental disorder in ways that make it differently frightening, because he can so easily hide his evil intent from those around him. Lecter can lure his victims into a sense of trust, making him a hidden threat rather than just an unpredictable one.

Hannibal Lecter (Anthony Hopkins) is an iconic character from the 1991 film directed by Jonathan Demme, while Ted Levine plays his serial killer foil, Jame Gumb. In *The Silence of the Lambs* a young detective, Clarice Starling, played by Jodie Foster, investigates a series of murders and abductions by a killer the FBI calls Buffalo Bill. The FBI later discovers that Buffalo Bill and Jame Gumb are the same person. These missing people include women who have vanished, been kept for days or weeks, and ultimately mutilated and killed. The FBI cadet Starling goes to Hannibal Lecter, an infamous psychologist and serial cannibal, for advice. Through the course of the investigation, Starling tempts and bribes Lecter to provide clues to help her catch the active serial killer.

Hannibal Lecter exudes a sophistication and class that encourage the spectators to engage with him despite his antisocial personality disorder. Anthony Hopkins brings with him a host of extra-cinematic references and associations that help to support his persona. From films like the 1968 *Lion in Winter*, 1980s *Elephant Man*, and a long series of Shakespearian works, Hopkins's filmography provides a pedigree and sophistication that many filmgoers would have known.[13] This level of cultural capital brought by the actor himself would have figured into his reception.

Along with Hopkins's history of performances, his accent and vocabulary evoke certain preconceptions in American audiences. The English accent in itself creates expectations of class and wealth for many Americans, and Hopkins plays upon those beliefs with his demeanor and mannerisms. He speaks the part of a smart man who can appear quite respectable. Even the "Dr." in front of his sophisticated sounding name, which evokes the teaching lectern, communicates his authority, knowledge, and class. All of these elements construct a figure audiences have been trained to trust, which makes his betrayal of that trust all the more grotesque.

When Starling first encounters Lecter, she walks slowly down a dungeon-like path with a barrage of inmates in cells to one side. The audience hears the lecture about how to behave around Lecter, which emphasizes his danger and his threat to her. The inmates in cells before Lecter proceed to catcall and harass her. They establish a baseline for the people with mental disorder in this place. They act in the stereotypical "crazy" ways that filmgoers expect. They meet the manic, loud, dirty, animalistic expectations of cinema's notion of mental disorder. After this barrage of angry men, Lecter appears in his cell standing courteously, if stiffly, waiting for Sterling's arrival. He politely says "please" and "thank you." Even when he uses innuendo to provoke her, by claiming that Jack Crawford is using her "student body," he does not speak crudely, only knowingly. He even places himself in contrast with the other inmate who asserted that he could "smell her cunt." He asserts, "I myself cannot. You use Evyan skin cream, and sometimes you wear L'Air du Temps, but not today." This maintains the sexuality of being able to smell her, but his comment does not sound dirty or gross, only rather intimate. He pushes boundaries, but he does not have the visceral physical markers of mental disorder that the audience sees in the other inmates, or that the Joker wears so overtly. As a serial killer who has antisocial personality disorder and therefore no empathy, he clearly experiences mental disorder while not seeming stereotypical to the audience at this time. Lecter's manners disguise his insanity and thus make him more dangerous. Like Patrick Bateman in *American Psycho*, the wealth, clothing, and posture of privilege provide him with enough cover and assuage others' expectations such that he appears mentally stable when not at that particular moment committing murder.[14] *The Silence of the Lambs* establishes a contrast between types of mental disorder; it puts Lecter in a position to seem relatable and dangerous but not understood as stereotypically like a person with a mental disorder, in contrast to Gumb.

Lecter's remark about Starling's appearance also locates him socially as observant and further undermines the cinematic stereotype of mental disorder. He looks at her and states, "Do you know what you look like, with your good bag and your cheap shoes?" He clearly knows what a "good bag" looks like as well as "cheap shoes." He is aware of social markers and can discern their literal and cultural value, which indicates that he comes from a high-class social situation. "You look like a rube. A well-scrubbed, hustling rube, with a little taste." His awareness of class places his position above hers, and his observational skills position him as dangerous and smart but not overtly mentally disordered.

Lecter's persona appears as sophisticated but also intimidating, which makes him like other cultural clichés about glamorous criminals. His infamy makes him a celebrated criminal akin to Robin Hood or Al Capone. He also arises before a strong trend of antiheroes in the last ten years like *Breaking Bad*'s Walter White, *The Sopranos*' Tony Soprano, or *Dexter*'s Dexter Morgan.[15] Lecter has a limited moral code, however twisted or ludicrous, which makes him respectable, despite his disregard for the law or human life. All of these features allow him to ultimately survive the cinema's imperative to destroy evil characters because his violent characteristics are superseded by his role as a white male elite. At the end of the film, he wanders off into the sunset after his nemesis, the warden. Lecter's performance reinforces the notion that Gumb's fall in the film does not result from his crimes, but other characteristics, in contrast with Lecter's sophisticated persona.

All of these elements of class, which allow Lecter to exist in this cinematic space, revere and celebrate him and become reversed in Buffalo Bill. Jame Gumb is a contrasting figure in tone, attire, affect, and accent. Even Gumb's name sounds awkward and evokes the idea of gum, which people chew and discard. Gumb appears unsophisticated and slovenly in comparison with Lecter. The contrast between the two characters occurs not in their willingness to murder or their mental disorders, but rather in their class and conformity to social and cultural conventions.

Gumb's role as the primary focus of the film's murder mystery creates a different kind of villain than Lecter, one that is much more unpredictable like the Joker. Gumb appears to be from a relatively low-income family in Belvedere, Ohio. The film shows this middle American town full of rundown homes, gray skies, and bare trees. Gumb's accent, mannerisms, posture, and clothing create a sense of a lack of class that appears in opposition to Lecter's. Gumb's clothing generally looks dull and cheap. He wears a torn blue T-shirt and later a brown polyester shirt that looks dated and unkempt. Most of his clothes demonstrate a lack of care or wealth that contrasts with Lecter's ironically pressed and fitted prison garb. These markers more easily align with the socially constructed notion of mental disorder, in part because mental disorder frequently comes with financial instability and thus markers of poverty or even homelessness. Gumb lacks Lecter's level of sophistication and taste, both markers of Lecter's cultural capital, so Gumb appears more severely mentally disordered than Lecter, despite their similar psychopathy.

During one scene in the film, Gumb puts on lipstick and eyeliner and wears a very effeminate and brightly colored robe. This occurs during the famous "tucked" scene, where Gumb has been seen putting on makeup, talking to no one, and dancing. Gumb then tucks his genitals between his legs, spreads the robes like butterfly wings, and looks in the mirror. The character's dressing in non-gender conforming ways in this robe and the later "woman suits," constructed from the skin of different women, are taboo for several reasons. The gender non-conforming clothes and rejection of traditional Hollywood masculinity break societal tropes. They undermine expectations and break rules. Even though the Hays codes had not operated for decades, they would have dictated that if a cross-dressing man was not comic relief, he would need to be punished for those cultural transgressions.

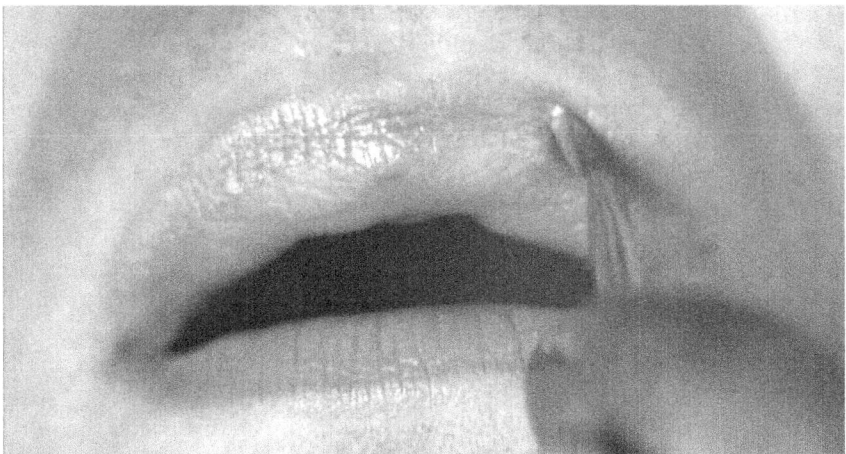

Figure 2.2. Jame Gumb applies lipstick in an extreme closeup. Jonathan Demme's 1991 *The Silence of the Lambs*.

Gumb's makeup aligns him with the Joker in the ways that their difference becomes something that they wear or put on that makes their mental disorder visible. These men in makeup serve, unfortunately, to villainize all men in makeup and correlate them with psychopathic behavior. This makeup and cover-up can serve to obscure and alter the images of these men. The element of discomfort encouraged by these men comes not from some inherent problem with makeup but the way the films establish these characters as grotesque in their disguises. Their inner problems become visually present in their efforts to alter their person. They need to obscure something in their own reflection, but the films represent this as evil rather than the characters' desire to physically express themselves. Their mental states become visible, and since they are both paired with extreme violence, their makeup or masks become tied to their instability and violence.

Most of the scenes where the audience sees Gumb appear as brief vignettes of Gumb's dark life. Most show clips of Gumb in his home, with special attention paid to the rundown condition and circumstances of his house. The scenes show clutter along with shabby decor and sad yellow lighting. The first view of Gumb's home is a long dolly shot as the viewer is pulled backward through tunnels that meander by tanks of insects, scary stone walls, Gumb sitting naked in a chair, and finally the dungeon in which he keeps his victims. During this long-shot reveal, the audience hears eerie music punctuated by Catherine Martin screaming in her well. This shows the film's implicit judgment of his living conditions and circumstances. He lacks the markers of cultural capital and class that Lecter exhibits despite Lecter's incarceration.

In conjunction with Gumb's lack of financial class, Gumb breaks social and cultural expectations, further undermining the character's standing. The film slowly reveals Gumb as a transgendered killer. Lecter describes Gumb as not a real transgendered person but a confused person who desires to "wear" a woman suit made by the victims. Despite Lecter's assertion that Gumb is not a "real transsexual," Gumb demonstrates markers that do indicate transsexuality for the audience. Even Lecter's denial of Gumb's own self-perception locates Gumb as being treated more like a traditional female character than a male character. Women's voices and opinions in classic Hollywood film are often dismissed or ignored as Lecter dismisses Gumb's desires or self-identification. America's phallocentric attitudes are visible in this gender-bending performance because an absolute gender binary is so culturally established. To defy these profound norms or resist cultural expectations locates Gumb as a transgendered Other.

At the time of its release, some LGBT communities protested the portrayal of a non-gender-conforming serial killer in *The Silence of the Lambs*.[16] The film showed an especially egregious representation when so few portrayals of people in the LGBT community had made it to film and television. Part of the audience's discomfort about Gumb may have been bolstered by their unfamiliarity with those in the transgendered community, especially through American mass media. By Gumb's break with expected behavior through nontraditional gender, any of the same kind of cultural capital that Lecter demonstrates becomes reversed in Gumb.

Somewhat ironically, Gumb operates as an aspiring femme fatale. Starling then is the hardboiled detective to Gumb's dangerous women. While not traditionally seductive in the same way as most femmes fatales, Gumb's feminine sexuality, power, danger, and the threat must be destroyed according to traditional Hollywood codes because of its social transgression and authority. Another characteristic includes the way that Gumb becomes a threat to a significant male character. This male character destroyed by Gumb is Gumb. This destruction of a male counterpart remains a hallmark of femmes fatales. The femme fatale also commonly breaks with expectations and social conventions, making Gumb dangerous and seemingly less sane.

Gumb represents a contemporary anxiety for the film's time. At the time of *The Silence of the Lamb*'s release in 1991, the general public understood very little about HIV or AIDS except that it could kill and it appeared to have a connection to the LGBT community. It remained largely mysterious and misunderstood, and that created anxiety and fear. According to Douglass Kellner in his chapter "Poltergeists, Gender and

Class in the Age of Reagan and Bush," "even conservative horror films reveal contemporary anxieties concerning the family, downward mobility, and homelessness in an uncertain economy and disintegrating social order." This notion of the horror film reflecting the anxieties of the time follows through to Gumb and the terrors that he represents in *The Silence of the Lambs*. Kellner also argues, "A subtext of these films is the confusion and fright of the population in the face of economic crisis; accelerating social and cultural change; a near epidemic of cancer, industrial diseases, and AIDS; political turmoil; and fear of nuclear annihilation." The horror films that Kellner discusses use contemporary tensions to compound the fundamental fears about the violence and death on-screen.

Gumb, like many femmes fatales, embodies an anxiety of the moment HIV/AIDS by being a person who does not conform to gender expectations. This community was at the heart of the HIV/AIDS epidemic, and the anxiety about this relatively new disease became embodied in the killer. Gumb goes out into the community, destroys women's bodies, injures "innocent" people, and does so without discriminating for class by capturing the senator's daughter. Even though Lecter claims that Gumb is not a "real transsexual," Gumb's clear refusal to gender conform connects him to the anxieties of the time for many audience members. Gumb breaks with social conventions and power structures, and classic Hollywood cinema's patterns of punishment resist allowing Gumb to survive like Lecter does.

Gumb and the Joker contrast with Lecter in the ways that they visually demonstrate difference from popular culture standards of mental stability and ideal masculinity. They wear their difference in ways that speak to the popular unconscious understanding of mental disorder and how it ought to be visible. The reality of people with mental disorder is that it comes in many different forms, is often not visible, and rarely comes with violence. However, these depictions play upon public anxieties about what the Other looks like and fears about what happens when one cannot see difference in the Other.

NOTES

1. "Mental Health Myths and Facts." *Mental Health Myths and Facts.* MentalHealth.gov (accessed March 27); and Human Services, April 22, 2018, https://www.mentalhealth.gov/basics/mental-health-myths-facts.

2. *Diagnostic and Statistical Manual of Mental Disorders: Fifth Edition* (Washington, DC: American Psychiatric Association, 2013).

3. Ibid.
4. Ibid.
5. Ibid.

6. *The Dark Knight*, dir. Christopher Nolan (2012; Burbank, CA: Warner Brothers, 2012), DVD.

7. *No Country for Old Men,* dir. Joel Coen and Ethan Coen. (2007; Los Angeles, CA: Miramax Films, 2007), DVD.

8. *Monster,* dir. Patty Jenkins (2003; Los Angeles, CA: DEJ Productions, 2004), DVD.

9. Kyra Pearson, "The Trouble with Aileen Wuornos, Feminism's "First Serial Killer." *Communication & Critical/Cultural Studies* 4, no. 3 (2007): 256–275.

10. *Batman Begins* dir. Christopher Nolan (2005; Burbank, CA: Warner Brothers, 2012), DVD; and *The Dark Knight Rises,* dir. Christopher Nolan (2012; Burbank, CA: Warner Brothers, 2012), DVD.

11. Jessecae Marsh and Lindzi Shanks, "Thinking You Can Catch Mental Illness: How Beliefs about Membership Attainment and Category Structure Influence Interactions with Mental Health Category Members." *Memory & Cognition* 42, no. 7(2014): 1011–1025. CINAHL Complete, EBSCO*host* (accessed May 4, 2018).

12. Jayci Robb and Jeff Stone, "Implicit Bias toward People with Mental Illness: A Systematic Literature Review." *Journal of Rehabilitation* 82, no. 4(2016): 9.

13. *Lion in Winter,* dir. Anthony Harvey (1968; Los Angeles, CA: AVCO Embassy Pictures); and *Elephant Man,* dir. David Lynch (1980; Los Angeles, CA: Brooksfilms).

14. *American Psycho,* directed by Mary Harron (2000; Los Angeles, CA: Muse Productions).

15. *Breaking Bad* (2008–2013; Albuquerque, NM: High Bridge Entertainment); *The Sopranos,* (1999–2007; New York); and *Dexter,* (2006–2013; Miami, FL: John Goldwyn Productions).

16. Kendall Phillips, "Consuming Community in Jonathan Demme's *The Silence of the Lambs,*" *Qualitative Research Reports in Communication* 1, no. 2 (2000): 26.

THREE
Cognitive Theory and Autism in *Rain Man* and *Mary and Max*

People with mental disorders that sometimes appear represented in film can serve as a pretext for displaying exceptionalism, such as Dustin Hoffman's character in the 1988 film *Rain Man* and his ability to count cards. Similarly, *The Wizard, Temple Grandin, The Girl with the Dragon Tattoo,* and *The Imitation Game* provide just a few examples of films that portray characters with varied mental disorder representing people on the autism spectrum and yet tell stories largely invested in their exceptionalism.[1] Conversely, other films operate as demonstrations of the benevolence of normates, such as the people around Cuba Gooding Jr.'s character in *Radio*.[2] This chapter examines two films, *Rain Man* and *Mary and Max,* through the lens of cognitive studies. I will directly analyze how their representations of disorder on film operate differently as vehicles to engage with a character who is on the autism spectrum. While these representations do identify characters as being on the autism spectrum, they, like any fictionalization, do not exactly mirror the referent or the person they are meant to be like.

Rain Man includes moral prescriptions for able-bodied neurotypical viewers, while *Mary and Max* works more directly to construct an engaging person on the autism spectrum. While many films about characters on the autism spectrum have come out since *Rain Man,* this film represents an iconic shift in people's awareness of the disorder.[3] *Rain Man* does not exert effort to engage the audience with its title character with a mental disorder but instead creates relationships that encourage the audience to pity Raymond (Dustin Hoffman) and engage with the surrounding normate characters. This particular film results in a highly moralized and condescending depiction that limits the characters with mental disorder to even more marginalized existences. Ultimately, I argue here that according to cognitive theory, *Rain Man* does not allow for engagement with Raymond because the condescension toward Raymond establishes him as a much less cognizant character than his ability implies. This subtle dehumanizing is problematic because audiences see it in different ways across other texts and because of the ways that representation shapes people's understanding of disorder and disability.

For the purpose of this chapter, I focus on two representations of people with autism as their similarities and character parallels provide a useful contrast for illustrating the sometimes problematic representations of these characters. Autism has become a popular topic in the media as issues such as the vaccine hoax and an increase in reported autism spectrum cases have arisen since the 1980s.[4] Television has recently incorporated more characters that it actively identifies as on the autism spectrum such as in *Scorpion*, *The Good Doctor*, and Netflix's *Atypical*.[5] Characters such as *The Big Bang Theory*'s Sheldon Cooper or *Bob's Burgers*' Tina Belcher also have traits that may indicate autism spectrum disorder.[6]

Disability appears on a spectrum that contains levels of disability and alternate mental disorders that do not allow for engagement as defined by Murray Smith's structure of sympathy. *Rain Man* and *Mary and Max* feature people with mental disorders that represent opposite approaches to character engagement. Despite superficial appearance, *Rain Man* does not support engagement with Raymond Babbit (Dustin Hoffman); in contrast, *Mary and Max* allows for cognitive engagement with the character of Max Jerry Horovitz as voiced by Philip Seymour Hoffman. The nuanced differences in the texts illustrate the substantial distinction between the two types of accessible representation.

Rain Man presents a fictional experience of two brothers who reconnect as adults and travel together across the country. Tom Cruise's character, Charlie Babbitt, discovers the existence of an autistic brother, Raymond Babbit, upon his estranged father's death. Charlie realizes that his father has made his brother heir to most of their father's considerable wealth. In Charlie's effort to reclaim control over the fortune, he kidnaps Raymond so that he can persuade Raymond's trustee to relinquish half of the inheritance. The brothers travel across the country in their father's prized convertible, stopping in Las Vegas to count cards and gamble enough money to pay off Charlie's debts. Ultimately, Charlie learns that Raymond requires more care than he can provide and returns Raymond to the care of his original institution. The film shows Raymond Babbitt as an autistic savant who, while socially and cognitively limited in some ways, has mathematical gifts including an ability to count cards. Ostensibly based on a real person's ability, the film fictionalizes the story of Raymond Babbitt and his adventure with his brother.

Raymond is a person on the autism spectrum who has lived in an institution for his entire adult life. His autism spectrum disorder and institutionalization limit his social abilities and makes him strongly averse to change. As Charlie realizes that Raymond can not only count items quickly but also perform other calculations rapidly, he uses Raymond's abilities to gamble in Las Vegas. Charlie's learning to love his brother regardless of his autism spectrum disorder and valuing his relationship more than the inheritance is the moral of the sentimental film. The film presents Raymond as a friendly character with pleasant eccentricities. However, that does not make him an engaging character.

In my analysis of Raymond as a character that the film structures as pitiable but not engaging, I am using the concept that is commonly understood as identification. I do not use the term identification; instead, I will implement the word engagement for the purposes of this chapter. While both terms do encompass many of the same notions of how spectators relate to characters, engagement does not carry with it the same psychoanalytic implications or the common usage, but it does encompass sympathy and empathy, as cognitivist theorists seek to avoid some previous theoretical entanglements. The term engagement also circumvents the theoretical implications raised by imagining oneself as another person. Murray Smith describes his application of the term engagement as a broader definition than identification, in proposing that "fictional narrations elicit three levels of imaginative engagement with characters, distinct types of responses normally conflated under the term 'identification.' Together, these levels of engagement comprise the 'structure of sympathy.'"[7] Smith critically engages with what he considers several of the misrepresentations that have arisen in understanding film identification. One such misconception about identification for him is the notion that spectators become one with the characters on screen.

Other understandings that Smith finds false include the belief that in identification a spectator "mistakes a representation for an actual referent."[8] Another is what Smith describes as the spectator "centrally imagining while never mistaking representation for referent."[9] Smith asserts, and I agree, that spectator relationships with characters arise through a structure of sympathy, which includes recognition, alignment, and allegiance. I find that these terms can help establish the parameters of spectator interactions with characters including those with mental disorder.

In the work *Engaging Characters*, Smith explains a structure for understanding spectators' relationships with characters on-screen, to establish which components of the cinematic experience can create the possibility of engagement. Smith develops what he calls a "person schema" to define what he believes will construct an engaging character. This schema includes seven different elements that make figures on-screen characters: a body; actions and self-awareness; intents, beliefs, and desires; emotions; language; self-impelled actions and self-interpretation; and traits. Smith proposes that recognition, alignment, and allegiance are the requirements for a character to establish the possibility of engagement. Smith bases his sense of recognition on at least a somewhat continuous recognizable figure that the spectator can identify as a particular entity. Alignment is a perspective that occurs when the spectator associates with a character for some portion of the film, which films accomplish through camera angles or narrative point of view. Allegiance includes the emotional connection to a character usually marked with sympathy, empathy, or dislike based largely on morality. However, while this schema may explain a character, it does not make a character engaging. Rather, the schema merely establishes the possibility of engagement.

The question of whether a character may be engaging begins with the notion of recognition. People with mental disorders easily reach this first hurdle of recognition. Characters with these mental disorders can easily be understood as a single, coherent, identifiable character. Spectators would not mistake Raymond, Max from *Mary and Max*, Sam in *Atypical*, or Temple from *Temple Grandin* as anything but clearly recognizable individuals. This notion of a single identifiable character might be questionable in a work like *Fight Club* as different parts of the same psyche appear as different actors with different names and characteristics. Yet, the two distinct portions of Jack/Tyler's psyche function cohesively within themselves and operate as individually recognizable, if not singular in their personhood.[10] Generally, given a particular name and cohesive appearance throughout the text, the preponderance of these characters with mental disorders easily meet the criteria of a recognizable character according to Smith's schema.

The second element of engagement, alignment, functions as a character arises from two primary factors, *spatiotemporal attachment* and *subjective access*. According to Smith, "Attachment is the function of narration which renders characters as agents, entities that act and behave; subjective access is the function that represents characters as entities that desire, believe, feel, think, and so forth."[11] Spatiotemporal attachment speaks to the way that the images and sound follow characters on screen. With eyeline matches, over-the-shoulder shots, and reaction shots of the characters, the film provides the viewer most of his or her information in relation to just a few characters in a film who, by virtue of the camera's attention, become the main characters. *Rain Man* primarily follows the life of Charlie. Even the title of the film, *Rain Man*, reflects Charlie's perspective of Raymond, rather than Raymond's understanding of himself. The film begins with Charlie doing business and encountering a financial crisis, which begins the rising action of the film. It also follows Charlie's revelation of the existence of his brother. The camera and the narrative reveal Charlie's perspective and journey. This physical relationship to a character like Charlie functionally develops out of cinema's visual structure; and thus, like recognition, it would not serve to meaningfully inhibit engagement with a person with even the most severe disability—although the greater the mental disorder, the less likely a text is to follow a character. Language skills are not necessary for engagement with a character, but characters without visible language skills are extremely rare as engaging figures. Exceptions include *Milo and Otis, Gromit,* and *Mr. Bean,* but they are not common.

Subjective access speaks to the "degree of access we have to the subjectivity of the character."[12] Smith follows this assertion with a question: "can we assume that all characters in all films have an inner life to the same degree and in the same sense? The structuralist tradition is right to insist that we cannot, although positing subjective access as a variable function in narrative should help us to move beyond this denial, toward a discrimination of the possible types of character subjectivity."[13] Smith asserts here that his schema functions by assuming subjectivity in ways that I argue do not clearly accommodate all of the variables for mental disorder or the audience's willingness to assume a character's subjectivity. He asserts that "positing subjective access" or assuming an engaging level of subjectivity makes characters people the audience can engage with. I am challenging the notion that cinema always creates the assumption of subjectivity about its characters. Not all characters on film are shown as moral subjects, not all spectators will presume a character's moral subjectivity, but more importantly, not all characters are shown to the audience as capable of being moral. While Smith may posit this moral subjectivity for characters as standard, not all films present characters so graciously. The fact that this subjectivity can be taken for granted reinforces how limited the typical representations on film are, and it demonstrates film's condescension that a figure like Raymond can appear without being engaging.

For a character in a film to be given the kind of alignment being discussed by Smith, the audience would have to assume that the character had a relatable level of subjectivity. While the narration, acting style, and music may inform the audience of the character's behavior and some of his or her desires, audiences must still assume a kind of similar subjectivity to themselves to follow through to an engaging relationship with a character. The characters in vegetative states in *The Awakening* would not be assumed to have subjectivity until given the drugs that wake them up. They cannot be aligned with as they are presumed to be noncognizant beings while in a coma. We do not think of them as feeling, reasoning people until they wake up. According to Smith's schema, they are no more engaging than a tree would be.

In terms of allegiance, Smith asserts that iconography factors into the audience's inclination toward engagement with a character: "The work of iconography in this respect, however, is omnipresent, and rapid: consider the way in which the conventional ugliness of the assassin in *The Man Who Knew Too Much* immediately fixes him as a suspicious character (frame 55). The effects of iconography range from very general assumptions embedded within cultures regarding, for example, racial types . . ."[14] Hollywood's predisposition against Others does not stop it from making a character like Raymond in *Rain Man* fully engaging as a lead character, but it does make that engagement improbable. Raymond exhibits particular mannerisms meant to appear autistic. Raymond was based on a real autistic savant, Kim Peek, and Hoffman modeled his mannerisms after him. Raymond's stiff posture, wringing hands, and awkward movements do mark him as different in ways that are quickly identifiable as Other. The film shows Raymond as markedly different than Tom Cruise's Charlie, who moves confidently and often arrogantly through the world. Even the choice of Tom Cruise, who had recently played several cool or sophisticated characters like Maverick in *Top Gun*, emphasizes the contrast in the brothers.[15] Raymond's wardrobe similarly locates him as somewhat childlike and awkward. Until Charlie buys him a suit, Raymond wears cheap K-Mart khakis and a jacket that look young and unsophisticated. The film shows Raymond as visually different in ways that do not necessarily stop engagement but may obscure or reduce it to some degree. While alliance does not stop Hollywood from creating engaging characters, common practice does make it more challenging and much less likely, according to typical Hollywood expectations for a lead character.

Murray Smith argues that the audience needs recognition, alliance, and allegiance to dictate whether a character has the possibility of being engaging. Recognition is relatively easy, and alliance is possible if less likely in classic Hollywood films' longstanding trends against commonly depicting positive characters who could be considered persons with a mental disorder. This leaves allegiance as the most significant problem with engagement. According to Smith's structure of sympathy, "To become allied with a character, the spectator must evaluate the character as representing a morally desirable (or at least preferable) set of traits, in relation to other characters within the fiction."[16] The character's actions or traits must be morally desirable or preferable to become a factor in his or her ability to be engaging. This stops the audience from engaging with the depiction of Raymond.

Allegiance requires that characters existing in relation to the moral system of Hollywood film must have the agency to be actively engaged in a moral issue such that they can be evaluated in terms of their morality. A person with a significant mental disorder may be below a threshold where he or she is making choices on a moral spectrum. In *Rain Man* Raymond nearly burns down Charlie's house by trying to cook. Raymond ignorantly puts a cardboard box in a toaster oven, which starts a small fire. This act would not be understood as a malicious or benevolent act by Raymond, but an innocent accident. Raymond does not actively make any moral choices that the audience has access to in the film. He appears similar to a very young child may act in ways that result in moral problems for another character, but not as one who makes moral choices himself. In contrast, an actual person similar to Raymond in ability and mental scope possibly may make these moral choices, but the film does not show Raymond making any moral choices; and as a fictional character, he only exists as the audience sees him on screen. If the film does not provide him with opportunities to make moral decisions, then the film does not construct him as a moral agent.

Murray Smith argues in an article "Gangsters, Cannibals, Aesthetes, or Apparently Perverse Allegiances" for an understanding of morality that is broad enough to encompass any number of apparently amoral situations or figures. In one example, Smith asserts that "accidents" in films such as *Pulp Fiction*, where an innocent person is accidentally killed with a shotgun, exist in a realm of moral implication that does inform the acts and makes them immoral. Rarely do good people in a movie accidentally shoot an innocent person. However, even if there are moral implications surrounding those acts in *Pulp Fiction* and other films with ostensibly amoral behavior, the films show numerous other acts that provide information or the characters are understood to be neurotypically subjective figures and thus responsible for situations where bad accidents happen, which allows the audience to feel repulsion or allegiance to a character.

Raymond cannot represent morally desirable traits if he does not have morality in the film. The kind of moral implication of the representation that appears in *Pulp Fiction* does give a sense that perhaps Raymond seems good because he does not act deliberately bad. This resembles the way that the characters in *Pulp Fiction* seem bad, based on the fact that generally only bad people point loaded guns at innocent people. The morality around Raymond and the film's perspective of Raymond make Raymond likable. The audience may even pity Raymond when he demonstrates anxiety at being asked to fly on an airplane. However, engagement requires more than pity or likability. A person can like and pity an infant in a film, but the audience is not asked to imagine what they would do in that body's position or relate to that infant's morality. There are, of course, exceptions like the 1990s Nickelodeon show *Rugrats*, which does feature infants as the central characters, but they talk, make decisions, and moral choices while merely looking like babies. Even animal characters that "star" in films typically do so as figures that the film either gives a literal voice or otherwise obvious moral agency beyond what the film supports Raymond having. Raymond is interesting, likable, pitiable, and nice but not a character we engage or identify with. While we may wonder what we would do in Charlie's position, we probably do not wonder what choices we would make if in Raymond's position. We do not imagine ourselves in Raymond's shoes because the film does not provide us with enough information to assume that Raymond's mental state operates meaningfully like most of us. The film does not encourage or promote the assumption that Raymond makes any moral choices. The idea of formal engagement requires more than likability. It is not a high bar for a film to achieve, and its lack is condescending.

Again, Smith argues that a character must "represent a morally desirable (or at least preferable) set of traits."[17] It seems unlikely that an inability to make moral choices would be desirable or preferable. Even the preferable traits that Raymond demonstrates in the film are actually Charlie's traits. In Murray Smith's chapter in Carl Plantinga and Greg M. Smith's book *Passionate Views: Film, Cognition, and Emotion*, Murray Smith describes how engaging Hannibal Lecter is in *The Silence of the Lambs* despite his immoral behavior, because he represents other traits that make him desirable or preferable in ways that override the audience's revulsion at his evil acts. Lecter appears as smart, classy, sophisticated, well spoken, and carefully dressed.

Raymond does have traits that might be argued to be "morally desirable," but I would assert that they do not easily fall into that category. Raymond could be argued to be smart in some ways, but not in a way relatable to most audiences. The film introduces Raymond's ability to see numbers and figures as foreign and abstract. Charlie seems surprised that Raymond knows the number of toothpicks on the floor. It is seemingly beyond understanding, like a magic trick. We do not get to hear how he thinks about these numbers or how he understands because the film is not ultimately interested in him as much as in his brother. Charlie's application of this skill to gambling, which could be understood in a moral context, was a choice made by Charlie rather than Raymond. Raymond did not understand the possible moral implications of card counting. This becomes obvious in a hearing where Charlie's ability to care for Raymond is being evaluated. Raymond tells the room that he and Charlie counted cards in Las Vegas. Nor does he recognize that there are moral implications to this statement. He does not recognize the implications of the interview. He does not demonstrate awareness of the morality of gambling or the possible consequences of telling the lawyers or arbiter. His ignorance is played for humorous effect, but it demonstrates his lack of awareness.

Charlie, in contrast with Raymond, functions as the moral center of *Rain Man* as his morality evolves and changes. Charlie's journey to become decent and ultimately to develop sympathy for Raymond gives us sympathy for Charlie. He begins the film as a self-centered man who lies to his clients and manipulates his girlfriend. He also has every intention of taking half of his autistic brother's inheritance. The film presents Charlie's actions as clearly immoral, but his journey leads him to the point of comprehension such that his priority becomes helping Raymond. This evolution operates as the emotional crux of the film. Raymond, in contrast, does not significantly change, despite his experiences with Charlie. In the director's voice-over on the 2014 DVD of *Rain Man*, the producer, Mark Johnson, states, "The movie is . . . it's about Charlie. The movie is about Charlie. It's not about Raymond because Charlie is the one who changes. And quite frankly that's why we go to movies. We don't go to see two people who remain the same."[18] Johnson states, almost apologetically, that this film does not focus on Raymond. Raymond, as shown by the film, appears incapable of the kind of moral growth that Johnson wants his Hollywood narrative to establish. This can be seen in other films about characters with mental disorders. When the film does not invest itself in the character's growth, it becomes a vehicle for the other figures' progress. For example, *Radio*, *The Soloist*, and *What's Eating Gilbert Grape* each present one character with a mental disorder, but the narrative arc examines the life of their caregiver.[19] In *Love Actually*, the person with a developmental disorder, Michael, appears largely as a burden on his sister's life.[20] Sarah picks her brother over a romantic relationship and demonstrates love and gives attention to her brother. Narratively, he is only an obstacle to her romantic relationships rather than a character who has his own narrative arc. This lack of growth or focus on Raymond does not mean that the audience does not find Raymond interesting or does not feel sorry for him.

In one scene, for example, when Raymond becomes anxious about the hot water in a bath, yelling "Hot water burn baby!" after recalling burning Charlie as a baby, the audience can easily feel sorry for him.[21] However, that kind of pity for a character does not necessarily raise him to the level of engagement that Smith defines. This pity connected with the lack of engagement does a disservice to the representations of people with mental disorders. Rather than placing people in a position on film that might engage the audience, films place people with mental disorders in a position where the audience feels paternalistic toward the characters. This condescending approach puts people with disabilities at a disadvantage. According to Michael T. Hayes and Rhonda S. Black, "Pity, as we have been arguing is much more than an emotional response, yet it is the emotional response that places the subject of pity, the viewer, into an asymmetrical power relationship with the object of pity, the disabled character."[22] This becomes a measure of control over people with a mental disorder.

As will be described further in the chapter on disability, Hayes and Black discuss how narratives establish this position of pity, and *Rain Man* clearly falls into their apparatus for understanding this work including the feeling of "social obligation" created as a means of controlling or confining people in ways that imply benevolence and charity on the part of the paternalistic or controlling party.[23] Raymond may have been better off returning to the institution than living with Charlie, but in the ways that the film conforms to this discourse of pity, they do not show the possibility of growth for Raymond that leaves this option open. Continued confinement remains the only option for Raymond and many cinematic representations of people with mental disorders.

Based on Smith's structure of sympathy, alliance is impossible if a character is truly amoral, but more significantly for a moral character with a significant mental disorder, alignment is improbable in a culture that devalues those who are not normates, and alignment is significantly inhibited if not entirely blocked by not being able to see a character make moral choices and not just the morality of those around them. This level of significant mental disorder represents a class of representations of people are not always given the agency to be engaging. My assessment of the amorality of a character criticizes the representation rather than the person. An example of representation that defies this patronizing option is *Mary and Max*. Max demonstrates characteristics that show moral choices and engagement, despite his diagnosis and several similar diagnostic characteristics that Max shares with Raymond.

Mary and Max is an example of a work that is part of a trend toward a more comprehensive representation of people on the autism spectrum. Perhaps it is the increase in people diagnosed on the autism spectrum, but advances have been made. Adam Elliot wrote and directed the 2009 animated Australian film *Mary and Max*. The film portrays the life of two unlikely pen pals who live a world apart. The eight-year-old Mary Daisy Dinkle (Bethany Whitmore) lives in Australia and suffers from bullying at school. It also becomes clear that her alcoholic mother and her distant father provide a less than ideal childhood. Her mother steals items from the store and post office, while her father spends his evenings working on his taxidermy in the garage. Mary finds Max Jerry Horovitz's (Philip Seymour Hoffman) name and address in an American phone book and decides to write him a letter. The forty-four-year-old Jewish Max lives in New York City and similarly struggles with social situations. Doctors in the film diagnose Max with Asperger's syndrome, which is a term that is used less today but is part of the autism spectrum. However, it is the term the character embraces.

The film navigates the two characters' relationship as it presents their respective miscommunications and struggles in a complex friendship. Max is an especially interesting character in that the film provides him with a central position despite his presentation on the autistic spectrum. His autism manifests itself partially through his extreme social anxiety. The character appears nearly nonverbal in his personal interactions, but he speaks to the audience through his narrated letters to Mary. In these letters, he does express his feelings and motives, and the audience hears his voice, which we never hear spoken to another character out loud. These letters between the characters serve as the contents of much of the voice-over narration in the film.

Max does not at first appear to be significantly more socially adept than Raymond in *Rain Man,* but because the film invests in his voice and point of view, the audience sees Max make moral decisions and choices. Despite the similarities in their presentations to the world, with the given information provided by each film, Raymond demonstrates a level of engagement below the threshold discussed by Smith, whereas Max does provide the level of moral choice that creates engagement.

Ironically, the film includes an event in Max's life that implies that he does not have the capability to make a moral judgment. During a hot summer, his air conditioner falls out of the wall, and it crashes onto a mime performing below his window. The mime dies, and the police apparently charge Max with his murder. The judge eventually dismisses the charges against Max. The film's narrator states, "Luckily, his manslaughter charges were dismissed because he was labeled mentally deficient."[24] The judge in the narrative clearly does not believe that Max has the mental capacity to understand the consequences of his actions; therefore, he could not be held liable for their consequences. The film never shows Max making this defense. Max appears on the witness stand looking terrified and not speaking. As all of his speech in the film occurs through his written accounts, the character may be nearly non-verbal in public. The film does not clarify this point, but since Max lives alone and goes to see a therapist, he probably speaks some. If he does not speak while under the stress of arrest, then the court could easily presume a higher level of incompetence than the audience hears through his voice from the letters. Despite the court's somewhat ironic ruling, however, some of Max's behavior proves that he does make moral choices and operates by a strict moral code.

Max and Raymond appear to have some issues in common. For example, they share a desire for order. Raymond likes his bed in hotels to be against the window. Max becomes infuriated by cigarette butts and littering in New York. He even makes a case for why people should not litter: "Last week I picked up 128 cigarette butts. People are always littering in New York. I do not understand why people break laws. Butts are bad because they wash out to sea and fish smoke them and become nicotine dependent. I am just joking because, of course, it is impossible for a cigarette to remain lit underwater. Also, fish do not have pockets to keep cigarette lighters in."[25] Max not only articulates the need to not litter because it is against the law, but he also makes the case that it harms fish populations. While he sets this up as a joke, his motivation for wanting cleanliness and order has morally significant environmental reasons. Raymond wants his bed to be up against the window because that is where it sat in his room at the institution. If Raymond has rational reasons for what he wants, for example, a good breeze or something aside from familiarity, the film does not provide it to the audience. The film does not bother to reveal Raymond's reasons for his choices or desires. Either way, the film does not provide the audience with any understanding of his motivations. He lacks the moral positions that Max has because in *Mary and Max* the film presents his voice to the audience in the form of the letters to Mary.

Figure 3.1. As Max describes his humorous rationale for why people should not throw cigarettes on the ground, we see what he has imagined. Adam Elliot's 2010 *Mary and Max*.

Later, when Mary writes a dissertation discussing Max and his autism spectrum disorder, the violation of his privacy makes him furious. He feels like she has betrayed the intimacy of their friendship. He then ignores her while her life falls into disarray. Eventually, he feels bad for ignoring Mary for so long and he forgives her. As reparations for his prolonged silence, he sends her his collection of figurines from their favorite cartoon. The letter to Mary, perhaps more effectively than the others, demonstrates his moral position in the film. He first establishes that the gift demonstrates his forgiveness, while clearly articulating his emotions. He discusses common emotions that most of us have felt when someone has hurt our feelings: "Dear Mary, Please find enclosed my entire Noblet collection as a sign that I forgive you. When I received your book, the emotions inside my brain felt like they were in a tumble dryer, smashing into each other . . ."[26] After proffering forgiveness, he outlines his rationale for his choice and demonstrates what he has learned.

> The reason I forgive you is because you are not perfect. You are imperfect, and so am I. All humans are imperfect, even the man outside my apartment who litters. . . . [Also] I would have to accept myself, my warts and all, and that we don't get to choose our warts. They are a part of us and we have to live with them. We can, however, choose our friends and I am glad I have chosen you. . . . You are my best friend. You are my only friend. Your American pen pal, Max Jerry Horovitz.[27]

Max learns from his relationship with Mary and from his psychologist. He grows to become a more complex character and a more compassionate friend. Through this process, he learns to accept Mary's flaws and forgive her, which shows a sophisticated thought process and emotional growth. Unlike the producer of *Rain Man,* Mark Johnson, who did not see an opportunity to have his autistic character grow and change, *Mary and Max*'s character Max grows and learns and demonstrates the kind of moral struggles that we all face. Max evolves to face obstacles more positively, and the moral is present for the audience as well.

The ultimate difference in Max and Raymond arises from the way that the two films show their autistic characters as moral agents. As Murray Smith outlines, some position or level of morality is a necessity for engagement; Max's ability to articulate his understanding of the world around him and his growth as a character make him an engaging character, despite many similarities with Raymond. The depiction of Raymond does not even seem to assume the possibility of growth, with the slight exception of Raymond's head bump with Charlie at the end of the film. This moment of familial affection hints at Raymond's feeling some affection for his brother, but that remains in the realm of feelings rather than morals. This moment is the closest he comes to being truly engaging. Raymond may be likable, but the film does not give him enough moral agency to make him relatable or ultimately engaging according to Smith's schema.

Ultimately, the pitiable position that Raymond appears in places him in a situation that Charlie, paternalistic and controlling, needs to save him from. Hayes and Black's discourse of pity not only clearly outlines how Raymond becomes pitiable, but how his continued containment as a character and the audience's understanding of him make him less empowering than a character like Max whose agency and self-awareness make him engaging and sympathetic in positive and compelling ways.

Rain Man demonstrates not how hard it would be to make a person with a severe mental disorder engaging, but rather how little it takes to make him engaging. Seeking to understand his motives, talking with characters who engage him in ways other than paternalistically, articulating his motivations, or centering the narrative on his evolution as well, would make Raymond a focus rather than a tool of the narrative. He serves his brother's narrative. The film even has the vehicle for Raymond's point of view in the photography that only appears in the credits. If rather than an afterthought at the end of the text Raymond's images had been featured to demonstrate or facilitate understanding him, then his views would have been considered. Instead, the film dismisses them. This chapter does not necessarily condemn all Hollywood films' depictions of people with a significant mental disorder, but it is critical of the way Hollywood film operates that can so easily dehumanize even a main character because of a lack of consideration of difference.

NOTES

1. *The Wizard,* dir. Todd Holland (1990; Los Angeles, CA: The Finnegan/Pinchuk Company); *Temple Grandin,* dir. Mick Jackson (2010; Santa Monica, CA: HBO Films); *The Girl with the Dragon Tattoo,* dir. David Fincher (2011; Los Angeles, CA: Scott Rudlin Productions); and *The Imitation Game,* dir. Morten Tyldum (2015; New York: The Weinstein Company).
2. *Rain Man,* dir. Barry Levinson (1988; Los Angeles, CA: United Artists, 2014), DVD; *Radio,* dir. Michael Tollin (2003; Santa Monica, CA: Revolution Studios, 2003), DVD.
3. Stuart Murray, *Representing Autism: Culture, Narrative, Fascination* (Liverpool: Liverpool University Press, 2008).
4. Ibid.
5. *Scorpion* (2014–2018; Los Angeles, CA: CBS Television Studios); *Atypical,* (2017; Culver City, CA: Sony Pictures Television); and *The Good Doctor,* (2017–2018; Culver City, CA: Sony Pictures Television).
6. *The Big Bang Theory* (2007–2018; Burbank, CA: Warner Brothers Television); and *Bob's Burgers* (2011–2018; North Hollywood, CA: Bento Box Entertainment).
7. Murray Smith, *Engaging Characters: Fiction, Emotion and the Cinema* (New York: Oxford University Press, 1995), 75.
8. Ibid.
9. Ibid.
10. *Fight Club.*
11. Smith, *Engaging Characters,* 143.
12. Ibid., 150.
13. Ibid., 150.
14. Ibid., 192.
15. *Top Gun,* dir. Tony Scott (1986; Hollywood, CA: Paramount Home Entertainment, 2011), DVD.
16. Smith, *Engaging Characters,* 188.
17. Ibid., 188.
18. *Rain Man.*
19. *The Soloist* and *What's Eating Gilbert Grape,* dir. Lasse Hallstrom (1993; Hollywood, CA: Paramount Pictures, 2013), DVD.
20. *Love Actually,* dir. Richard Curtis (2003; Universal City, CA: Universal Pictures, 2003), DVD.
21. Ibid.
22. Michael T. Hayes and Rhonda S. Black, "Troubling Signs: Disability, Hollywood Movies and the Construction of a Discourse of Pity," *Disability Studies Quarterly* 23, no. 2 (2003).
23. Ibid.
24. *Mary and Max.*
25. Ibid.
26. Ibid.
27. Ibid.

FOUR

Disability Theory and Race in *Radio* and *The Soloist*

The films *Radio*, directed by Michael Tollin, and *The Soloist*, directed by Joe Wright, serve as two works in a very small category of feature-length American Hollywood films that have lead characters who are both people of color and have clearly indicated mental disorders. Because of the convergence of factors, these films illustrate the intersectionality of representations of race and disability. The "white savior film" as described by Jamie Schultz and others addresses the racial power structures at play in the work. These films' structure and form closely resemble the "discourse of pity" as theorized by Michael T. Hayes and Rhonda S. Black about people with disabilities. I argue that both sets of narrative parameters about race and disability overlap in explaining some of the ways that classic Hollywood cinema tells stories about people outside the spectrum of the white male normate. Hollywood film often deals with Others in ways that ensure that they appear controlled and palatable for the consumption of their presumed audience. The films' representations of the two nonwhite characters with mental disorders function in aspirational or hopeful narratives that ostensibly celebrate helping the less privileged. However, both films suffer from classic Hollywood formulas that establish frequently condescending perspectives and dehumanizing representations.

Radio and *The Soloist* use pity and fear to locate characters as infantilized figures that, unlike Raymond, are engaging, according to Murray Smith's schema, but the "discourse of pity" as outlined by Hayes and Black's article keeps these black men with mental disorders from being agents of their own narrative. I argue that this structure of pity explains many of the features of how these characters are represented. The structure of pity, despite being theorized for disability studies, also explains the way that people of color are represented in white savior films like *Radio* and *The Soloist*. These theoretical understandings of representation address the ways that white male normate figures in film reinforce their control and authority over people with mental disorder and non-white characters. These techniques operate as a means of control and subjugation.

Despite being the title characters, neither *Radio* nor *The Soloist* shows Radio (Cuba Gooding Jr.) or Ayers (Jamie Foxx) as leading the primary narrative arc, controlling the action, or telling their own stories. I argue that the director and writers of Radio's narrative superseded Radio's story with that of his white coach for the exact reasons discussed in the chapter on *Rain Man*. The producers did not see Radio as a character who could grow or evolve in useful narrative ways for the traditional Hollywood story line. Nor did the filmmakers encourage the audience to find the character very relatable, even though he does pass the threshold of being engaging through his charity work and a few other scenes where he makes clearly moral decisions. While a star performer enacts a remarkable change of fate for this man, the story does not primarily tell of his suffering, angst, or growth. These are mere subplots in *Radio*. *The Soloist*, in contrast, communicates much more of Ayers's story and spends more time and effort to establish Ayers's perspective. However, his narrative still remains subsumed under the growth and narrative arc created by Lopez as played by Robert Downey Jr. The reasons for Hollywood's choices in these films appear as an indictment of their willingness to represent both people with mental disorder and people of color.

Both African Americans and people with mental disorder have historically been seen as threatening to the able-bodied white establishment in American film. The notoriously racist *Birth of a Nation* is the obvious early example of how that perceived threat to white America was portrayed in film.[1] Similarly, people with a mental disorder have often been shown to be dangerous and threatening as villains such as Hannibal Lecter and Jame Gumb, or even Captain Hook or Darth Vader. While *Radio* and *The Soloist* are two exceptions, others do exist in less than full-release Hollywood works. Jennifer Hudson plays an African American woman with PTSD in *Call Me Crazy*, a Lifetime movie.[2] Halle Berry plays a woman with multiple personality disorder in *Frankie and Alice* and a woman who believes she may have gone crazy in *Gothika*, although that film ultimately turns into a ghost story. Both minorities and people with disabilities have often been relegated in American film to the periphery through oppressive and controlling representations.

While I am arguing that the intersection of African Americans and people with a mental disorder on screen elucidates certain similarities between their representations, this comparison has historically been fraught. According to Josh Lukin in his work "Disability and Blackness," the intersection between blackness and disability has been problematic:

"Simply put, from the beginnings of the United States, the claim that 'blackness is like disability' was not used as an expression of how black Americans suffered but as a tool of their own oppression."[3] Lukin argues that the implication that either group's problems could be simplified or reduced to "a metaphor" for the problems or concerns of the other group created tension. One such example might be May in *The Secret Life of Bees*. She is seemingly a positive figure with a mental disorder, but with her eventual suicide, she plays a part that does a great deal to move the other characters forward more than she serves herself. She might also fit into the role of the "magical negro," as an African American stereotyped character who comes into the narrative and speaks wisdom to help the white protagonist, according to Mathew Hughey in "Racializing Redemption, Reproducing Racism: The Odyssey of Magical Negroes and White Saviors." He describes the term: "From the darker bon sauvage ('Noble Savage') character of 17th century French literature, to the 19th century White 'settler' of Manifest Destiny propaganda, racialized saviors have grown into distinct and racialized film characters. The Magical Negro is a mysterious Black character that enters a decidedly White and mainstream context. This character labors to transform the life of a lost and broken White character that has somehow fallen from social and moral grace."[4] I do not argue that the experiences of people in either group are the same. I argue that both people with a mental disorder and African Americans have some similar representations on film that reflect an oppressive culture's efforts to control them through pity and an effort to make them more safe or palatable for stereotypical white normate audiences. As both categories are socially constructed hierarchical concepts, it is not surprising that their treatment by film has distinct similarities. While Hollywood cinema typically underrepresents African Americans and people with mental disorders, the representations of them frequently appear problematic.

In Hayes and Black's article "Troubling Signs: Disability, Hollywood Movies and the Construction of a Discourse of Pity," they outline the parameters of the "discourse of pity" that they see in the representations of those with a disability in Hollywood film: "When viewed from this perspective, disability is a set of signs and symbols that are articulated through the discourse of pity into the context of the film's characters, plot, and setting. It is, in fact, only through the articulation of these signs and symbols that people with disabilities are afforded an existence in Hollywood movies."[5] They outline how films structure narratives that leave the person with a disability in a marginalized state. Typically, these figures are treated paternalistically by other characters and the narrative itself. The figures with a disability function as a symbol of the primary characters' growth or development, rather than an independent character around whom the narrative could be centered. This holds true for both *Radio* and *The Soloist*.

Inspired by a true story, *Radio*, directed by Michael Tollin, tells the story of a coach who befriends and mentors a man with a developmental disorder. Coach Harold Jones played by Ed Harris, notices a young man, James Robert Kennedy, known as Radio. The film shows Radio's seemingly aimless life as he pushes a grocery cart around a small Southern town. Coach Jones sees Radio around the football field and helps rescue him from some bullying by the football players. Jones begins to include Radio in activities like attending games, helping at practice, and participating in many school functions. Jones provides him with attention, and ultimately Radio becomes a volunteer assistant to the football team. The climax of the movie occurs as Coach Jones must defend his inclusion of Radio in the team's activities and on the school grounds. Jones stands in front of a barbershop full of men and women after a lost game. They question the coach's choice to focus so much energy on Radio, perhaps at the expense of the team or their students. Coach Jones makes an argument for compassion and inclusion that seemingly wins over the crowd. The story, while called *Radio*, follows Coach Jones's journey of getting to know Radio and defending his choice to invite a man with a developmental disorder to participate with the team.

Disability theorists like Rosemarie Garland Thomson have made the argument that disability, like gender and race, involves socially constructed concepts rather than clear, identifiable divisions between people's different experiences. There is no distinct or obvious point when an able-bodied person becomes disabled, but rather a more liminal space that is nearly impossible to define. To establish a clear point between the concepts of able-bodied and disabled, one would have to create a degree of mobility, a specific IQ, a duration of the condition, and other variable factors which nuance and experience would necessarily complicate. Hayes and Black take a Foucauldian approach to the notion of discourse as "socially produced ways of talking about an object that situate the object within socially produced relations of power."[6] Hayes and Black, as well as other disability theorists, point out the lack of a precise mark or level of disability that leaves a person disabled in the same way that there is no absolute divide between black and white Americans.[7] Rosemarie Garland Thomson states in her book that she wants to "challenge entrenched assumptions that 'able-bodiedness' and its conceptual opposite, 'disability,' are self-evident physical conditions. My intention is to defamiliarize these identity categories by disclosing how the 'physically disabled' are produced by way of legal, medical, political, cultural, and literary narratives that comprise an exclusionary discourse."[8]

Laws and social rules often emphasize and exaggerate these lines or divisions between people, such as the one-drop rule for African Americans in the South during slavery and segregation. There is no biologically distinct divide between races of people. Only the socially constructed rules and laws create divides between races or those with and without a disability. Thomson goes on to say, "Disability, then, is the attribution of corporeal deviance—not so much a property of bodies as a product of cultural rules about what bodies should be or do."[9] I would include here that this notion of what a body should "be or do" also includes what it looks like, how it performs, and how it is treated on-screen. There is no line or divide between people with disabilities and normates despite the socially constructed division in most film.

The film *Radio* is a point of convergence between the social construction of race and disability. The character Radio is both African American and a person with a developmental disorder. These two factors serve to conflate and layer the issues that face nonwhite characters with developmental disorders. Unfortunately, this convergence comes with stigma and condescension from both characters in the film and the structure of the film itself.

Radio is an example of what Jamie Schultz calls "White Savior Historical Sport Film[s]" that, while ostensibly about black athletes, actually focus on white figures that raise the black athletes out of their downtrodden circumstances. She argues, "It is a rehabilitated, populist narrative that recapitulates the nineteenth-century ideology of the 'white man's burden.'"[10] Schultz states that these films serve as condescending narratives that primarily celebrate a white lead at the expense of placing the nonwhite athletes in a position of being needy and incapable of helping themselves. The white character then must help the nonwhite athletes as a type of charity and because of pity. While Schultz does not discuss *Radio* extensively, she does mention the film in this category. The notion that the film tells the story of a white man who helps "save" a black man is compounded by the way that it also tells a story of a normate man who helps "save" a developmentally disabled man. The choices in this film lead the audience to follow and engage primarily with the white normate figure and guide them to pity the black man with a developmental disorder. According to Tobin Siebers, "Many representations of people with disabilities, however, use narrative structures that masquerade disability to benefit the able-bodied public and reinforce the ideology of ability."[11] This dynamic between the helper and the helped reinforces arguments that notions of disability serve to keep the disabled "needy" and to reaffirm the power dynamics through social constructions.

This film primarily engages with Coach Jones, the "white savior." The predominance of camera angles, the point-of-view shots, and the narrative tell the story of how Coach Jones discovers Radio, fights for him, and helps him. The film does begin by introducing Radio to the audience who sees Radio pushing a grocery cart down a railroad track and listening to a portable radio. They then hear a voice-over by the coach's wife. She states, "Here in the upstate, things don't change much. Fall means football season. Being married to a coach means measuring things mainly by wins and losses . . . except for that one year." Her words, while implying that there is something important about the person on screen, mostly discuss the experience she and her husband have that year. The next shot shows Radio riding in his grocery cart down a hill. While these first few minutes offer a brief window into the life of Radio and his experiences, the audience's focus on and access to Radio lessens immediately after the first shot of Coach Jones. As soon as the narrative about Coach Jones begins, just a few minutes into the film, it becomes about how the coach learns to become compassionate and caring for Radio, rather than about Radio's experience of his time with the football team. Radio also spends time with others at the high school, makes new friends, and participates in other school activities. Finally, Radio's friendship with the coach changes him and how he interacts with others. Radio moves from being a recluse who speaks to no one but his immediate family to an extrovert known and embraced by the entire town. The true story, on which the narrative was based, contained a wealth of material from which the film could have relayed more of Radio's story and growth as a character.

After Radio's first visual sequence, the film primarily follows Coach Jones home to his family and his story of the football season. For the first third of the film, Radio largely lurks at the perimeter of each scene. Radio appears in long shots that make him look small behind numerous chain-link fences while clutching a football but not speaking and seldom being spoken to. The film shows Jones's family, follows his discussions with the administration, and portrays him rescuing Radio after some football players attacked him. The audience does not witness the assault by the players or Radio's experience of the encounter, only the moment that Jones finds him. One might assume that a film titled *Radio* would follow such a moment of emotional turmoil, as the football players kidnapped, tied up, and harassed him in a tool shed. The film does not show Radio's pain because the film is not invested in his story of growth or good fortune, but rather the coach's story of finding him. However, as with *Rain Man*, this work does not often ask the audience to engage with Radio beyond the establishment of a paternalistic pity. The film aligns us with Jones, and most audience members would probably wonder how we would act in his place, not how we would feel if we were like Radio. The film's primary alignment follows the white normate coach.

At the climax of the film, Coach Jones argues for the importance of including Radio in the activities of the school and town. This appears disappointingly ironic in a movie that could have included Radio more extensively. Jones justifies including Radio by asserting that he succeeds at being nicer than any of the other people in town. Tobin Siebers addresses this motif as what he calls the myth of the "supercripple." He describes how in different films "In other words, the hero is—simultaneously and incoherently—'cripple' and 'supercripple.'"[12] Like Raymond's ability to count cards, Coach Jones and the film ascribe to Radio a skill which he can provide more effectively than anyone else. His "skill" as described by Jones includes being "nicer" than anyone else, but this still functions to make him condescendingly exemplary.

By foregrounding this scene where Coach Jones justifies Radio's treatment as the climax of the work, the film makes apparent how Coach Jones must explain Radio's value to the community and to the films audience, because Radio's value as a person is not inherently given. Jones does not assert that people should behave nicely toward Radio because people should always behave decently, or that they should consider Radio's emotions. Instead, Jones argues that Radio provides the townspeople value in his niceness. This condescending move by the film makes Radio's worth as a person attributable to his friendly demeanor and his value to others, rather than his inherent humanity. This also implies that if Radio were not the friendliest person in town, they would have no obligation to treat him decently.

If *Radio* is as a point of convergence between issues of representation of race and disability, it also raises the issue of casting. Radio was played by Cuba Gooding Jr., a neurotypical African American man who portrays an African American man with a significant mental disorder. This casting becomes problematic for some critics, as a person with a disability could have performed this role in the film. Tobin Siebers makes an argument about Dustin Hoffman's performance as both a woman in *Tootsie* and also a person on the autism spectrum in *Rain Man*: "In short, when we view an able-bodied actor playing disabled, we have the same experience of exaggeration and performance as when we view a man playing a woman."[13] Siebers makes the point that the performance of a person who has a different lived experience would result in an exaggerated performance in an effort to enact the signs or indicators of gender, or in this case disability.

Siebers also states that casting a normate as a person with a disability "renders disability invisible because able-bodied people substitute for people with disabilities, similar to white performers who put on blackface at minstrel shows or to straight actors who play 'fag' to bad comic effect."[14] Siebers speaks to the typical exaggeration of figures who perform an identity in addition to performing an individual. Three primary concerns arise with blackface which surface in similar ways to a normate performing as a person with a disability or normate-face. The first concern arises because blackface has the historical baggage of minstrel shows and the negative representations and stereotypes of people of color. People with disabilities have been mocked and used humorously by performers as idiots or fools, so mocking them now may have a similarly negative resonance as mocking a person for the color of his or her skin. The second element that arises when using blackface occurs because it takes opportunity away from people of color and gives that job and opportunity to a white person. This same concern continues as people with disabilities would similarly be denied a job given to a normate. The third concern is the idea that Siebers mentions that the blackness or disability becomes a performance of identity, where an actor does more than pretend to be a person but pretends to enact the embodiment of a person with a disability. This could easily become mocking but also gives a false impression of how someone with that disability would actually behave. There are numerous parallels in the ways that representations of African Americans and people with disabilities typically fail to establish characters beyond pity or oppression.

The challenges with the representation seen in *Radio* can be understood as issues of the representation of both people of color and those with a disability. *Radio* tells a white savior story through the discourse of pity established by Black and Hayes.

> Paternalism attempts to mask relationships of domination and subordinance within a sense of benevolence that is bestowed on the subordinate by the dominant. The film's narrative paternalism is enacted at two mutually reinforcing levels: (a) the disabled are remanded back to the care of another, and (b) the viewer is inserted through the emotional response of sadness or sorrow. In both cases, the relationship of domination and subordination is clouded by an illusion of benevolence.[15]

While the paternalism in *Radio* appears rather overtly as the relationship of the coach to Radio, the results of that dominant and subordinate relationship reinforce it as benevolent and charitable. Another cinematic example includes *The Blind Side,* where an African American sports star is raised and supported by a white family. Similarly, *Freedom Writers, Dangerous Minds*, and *Cool Runnings* all present white characters who save the people of color.[16] The condescension and structures of control designed to appear benevolent to people of color in white savior films mirror the cinematic manipulation of those with a disability. Both groups are spoken down to in these formulaic texts in ways that control and limit the representations of Others. While many of these problems exist in other films, *Radio* presents them more overtly than some other works, including *The Soloist.*

Based on the memoir by Steve Lopez, *The Soloist* tells the story of Lopez and his relationship with the schizophrenic, homeless man, Nathaniel Ayers. While Lopez does have a Hispanic surname, the Caucasian performer, Robert Downey Jr., plays Lopez and speaks, looks, and for all cinematic purposes operates as a white man. I will refer to the character as white or Caucasian, as based on the performance that the audience sees. The recently divorced Lopez works as a columnist at the *Los Angeles Times* and finds himself struggling to create stories for his column. While working on a different story, Lopez comes across an apparently homeless man playing a violin with two strings. Lopez learns that Ayers once attended Juilliard and plays cello very well. Ayers also appears to have either schizophrenia or something similar to it, although the film makes an effort to question the usefulness of his or other mental health diagnoses for many of the homeless. Lopez spends most of the film trying to give Ayers access to a quality instrument, opportunities to perform in a concert hall, and ultimately an apartment. Ayers's schizophrenia repeatedly interferes with the seemingly logical and beneficial opportunities that Lopez tries to provide, but Ayers ultimately agrees to live in the apartment. Lopez finishes the story uncertain whether he has effectively helped Ayers, but Lopez believes that he has become a better person for their interactions.

The film clearly establishes itself as told from the perspective of Lopez. The film begins by watching Lopez crash his bike and tell his story about experiencing the overcrowded emergency room. Lopez's voice serves as the film's narrator, and it echoes elements of the actual columnist's articles about Ayers and himself. The character of Lopez voices his reactions and understandings of his relationship with Ayers as well as his perspective of these events. The film also emphasizes Lopez's narrative arc of meeting, knowing, and accepting Ayers. The moral that the voice-over gives at the end of the story articulates how Lopez has come to feel about their relationship and clearly states the point of the story to the audience:

> A year ago, I met a man who was down on his luck and thought I might be able to help him. I don't know that I have. Yes, my friend Mr. Ayers now sleeps inside. He has a key. He has a bed. But his mental state and his well-being are as precarious now as they were the day we met. . . . I can't speak for Mr. Ayers in that regard. Maybe our friendship has helped him. But maybe not. I can, however, speak for myself. I can tell you that by witnessing Mr. Ayers's courage, his humility, his faith in the power of his art, I've learned the dignity of being loyal to something you believe in. Of holding onto it, above all else. Of believing, without question, that it will carry you home.[17]

Lopez tells the audience that this story is about what he has learned from Ayers. He has become better because of watching Ayers. He has evolved as a person through their relationship, and the closing words in this film inform us that this film is about Lopez's journey. Despite his voice-over reinforcing the understanding that this is Lopez's story and not Ayers's, the narration does the positive work of not assuming Lopez knows how Ayers feels. Lopez clearly states, "I can't speak for Mr. Ayers in that regard."[18] This does not dismiss Ayers's opinion as irrelevant or assume that Lopez knows what is good for Ayers. What it does not do is tell the audience what Ayers thinks from Ayers's perspective. He is not given a voice here. While Ayers's voice is acknowledged, which moves it beyond what *Radio* accomplishes for Radio, the film still leaves Ayers voiceless about the primary arc of the film.

The Soloist improves upon *Radio*'s representation in several ways. The primary effort that *The Soloist* makes is in the time invested in telling Ayers's story over Radio's. *The Soloist* includes brief flashbacks throughout the film about Ayers's childhood and youth. These flashbacks begin by showing a young Ayers auditioning for a new cello teacher. However, as the story sets up the flashback, it becomes clear that the flashback arises from the memory and words of the cello teacher rather than from Ayers himself. The voice of the teacher narrates the images on-screen. Lopez called the people in Ayers's past to inquire about Ayers's history. Another white man tells Ayers's childhood story for him. A second flashback comes from Ayers's sister as she recalls some of his erratic behavior that arose during his time at Juilliard. While his sister appears at the end of the flashback as the teller of this story, within the flashback the audience hears the voices in Ayers's head. The voices echo around him about feeling judged and watched. We hear, "You'll never get out of here" and "They'll see you, Nathaniel."[19] Ayers's paranoid voices become a soundtrack to his experiences. This move by the director, Joe Wright, to insert these voices for the audience attempts to give the viewers Ayers's point of view. We hear the voices that bother Ayers, and along with tense, dark music, we can feel some small measure of his distress. By locating this part of the film from Ayers's point of view, Wright seeks sympathy and engagement with the audience for Ayers. This effort to invest in Ayers's point of view makes *The Soloist* a more equitable and positive narrative in terms of its representation than *Radio,* but the limited time spent on Ayers as compared to Lopez keeps the film from improving further.

Another element of the film that attempts to move us toward engagement with Ayers occurs in the scene where Ayers and Lopez watch the Los Angeles Philharmonic rehearse. Because Ayers fears to disrupt a traditional concert, Lopez provides the opportunity for the two of them to see a concert rehearsal. The scene shows the philharmonic begin to play but cuts to Ayers and Lopez as they watch the performance. Ayers appears enraptured by the music. He sways and murmurs and smiles gently during the concert. Lopez stops watching the philharmonic to observe Ayers have fun and revel in the sound. Much like parents watch their children enjoying an event or occasion, Lopez enjoys the concert by appreciating Ayers's joy. The scene also shows colors and flashes of light that presumably represent Ayers's experience of the music. However, Lopez's observation of him feels paternalistic. After the concert Lopez tells his ex-wife Mary Weston, played by Catherine Keener, about the experience:

> I'm telling you, it was such an unbelievable experience, the whole thing, the whole day. And if you had seen him, if you could have felt him. . . . I mean, it's the same hall. We're listening to the same goddamn music, but. . . . But no. You see him, it's one thing, but you feel him. . . .

I'm watching him. He's watching the music. And while they're playing, I say, "My God, there is something higher out there. Something higher out there, and he lives in it, and he's with it." I've never even experienced it, but I can tell... I don't even know what you fucking call it.[20]

Mary's response to his rant is to call the feeling "grace."[21] This discussion elaborates on the scene where Lopez watches Ayers listen to the music.

The narrative spends more time listening to Lopez's opinion about Ayers than Ayers's point of view. The narrative does not trust the audience to understand the joy and jubilation of Ayers, so it spends time having Lopez explain his joy to us. Audiences are not expected to relate directly to the schizophrenic Ayers, so his joy must be articulated by his white normate translator. This does not give the audience enough credit to assume that they would understand his joy by just watching Jamie Foxx, an Academy Award-winning actor. The film could have also spent more time watching Ayers. The light could have swirled around him, the music could have become progressively louder, and the camera could have slowly zoomed closer and closer to an extreme close-up. There are many cinematic choices that could have invested the audience in Ayers, but the effort was minimal because Lopez explained it to us. By not giving Ayers the ability to tell his own story, but by giving it to Lopez, it undermines Ayers's voice and point of view in the text. This is a key factor in the white savior narratives and how they use the story of an African American person as told or relayed through the perspective of a white performer. Audiences who are largely presumed to be white normates are not trusted to engage in a nonwhite person with a mental disorder.

Despite *The Soloist*'s progress toward some agency with Ayers, the narrative fits neatly into Hayes and Black's discourse of pity: "In Hollywood films the discourse of pity articulates disability as a problem of social, physical and emotional confinement. The disabled character's thwarted quest for freedom ultimately leads to remanding the character back to the confines of a paternalistic relationship of subordination."[22] As Ayers moves from his location on the streets to live in an apartment, he follows through the four parts of Hayes and Black's discourse of pity as they outline it: "In Hollywood films a discourse of pity frames the structure of the narrative into four inter linked parts: (a) confinement, (b) hope for rehabilitation, (c) denial of rehabilitation, and (d) reconciliation of confinement. Individually and together these elements situate disability into a network of paternalistic power relations that confines those with disabilities and articulates confinement as a social obligation."[23] Ayers goes through each of these steps. The final part is his "reconciliation of confinement" as Ayers accepts his new apartment provided by Lopez.[24] The apartment represents a new limitation to Ayers that he initially resists. He does not want the confinement of the apartment but accepts it by the end of the film. Ayers also comes to trust and rely on Lopez, which places him in a position of authority over Ayers. Lopez calls them friends, but the relationship does not appear equal as Lopez continues to place his judgment above Ayers, concerning Ayers's life.

Lopez clearly assumes that Ayers would have a happier or better life in a shelter or living inside. While Ayers eventually does decide to stay in the apartment, Lopez does not seem to accept that Ayers might know that sleeping on the street might be better than a crowded shelter for Ayers's life or his mental state. According to Hayes and Black, an element of the discourse of pity is the way that "paternalism assumes that an individual or group does not have the capacity to make life changing decisions and that those decisions must be made by a caretaker or overseer (Sartorius 1983). The caretaker or overseer can be an individual (relative, employee) an institution. . ."[25] In Lopez's final speech, the film hints at the possibility that Ayers does not have a better life, but the overall narrative of Lopez's saving Ayers does imply that Lopez's answers remain better than Ayers's.

While *The Soloist* does communicate Ayers's perspective more effectively than *Radio* provides Radio's point of view, *The Soloist* still places Ayers in a pitiable position rather than a place where the audience will likely identify with him. The film encourages the audience to feel sorry for Ayers much more often than it encourages it to identify with his struggles, loves, or choices. The film operates as a more nuanced "white savior film," but it continues to serve as a discourse of pity in the way that it approaches Ayers's mental disorder

Radio and *The Soloist* are ostensibly about Radio and Ayers the soloist, but neither narrative focuses on the title character. The films approach more familiar cinematic white male normate leads to provide the narrative arc and to create presumably more easily relatable main characters. These filmmakers assume that audiences will not relate to these black non-neurotypical men, even though film is an incredible medium to create psychological attachment and relationships with strangers onscreen. Unfortunately, this lack of faith in the spectator's ability to relate to these men leaves a condescending narrative that works to reinforce their control and oppression. Both films construct structures that serve to contain or control the Other in ways that make them "safe" for the consumption of large audiences through pity or restraint. The narratives primarily tell the story of their "white saviors" at the expense of their title characters.

NOTES

1. *Birth of a Nation,* dir. D. W. Griffith (1915; David W. Griffith Corp).

2. *Call Me Crazy*, dir. Laura Dern, Bryce Dallas Howard, and Bonnie Hunt (2013; WA: Echo Films).

3. Josh Lukin, "Disability and Blackness," in *The Disability Studies Reader*, ed. Lennard J. Davis (New York: Routledge, 2013), 313.

4. Mathew Hughey, "Racializing Redemption, Reproducing Racism: The Odyssey of Magical Negroes and White Saviors," *Sociology Compass* 6, no. 9 (2012): 751–67.

5. Michael T. Hayes and Rhonda S. Black, "Troubling Signs: Disability, Hollywood Movies and the Construction of a Discourse of Pity," *Disability Studies Quarterly* 23, no. 2 (Spring 2003).

6. Ibid.

7. Thomson, *Extraordinary Bodies*.

8. Ibid., 6.

9. Ibid.

10. Jamie Schultz, "Glory Road (2006) and the White Savior Historical Sport Film," *Journal of Popular Film & Television* 42, no. 4 (October 2014): 205–13.

11. Tobin Siebers, *Disability Theory* (Ann Arbor, MI: University of Michigan Press, 2008), 111.

12. Ibid.

13. Ibid., 115.

14. Ibid., 116.

15. Hayes and Black, "Troubling Signs."

16. *Freedom Writers*, dir. Richard LaGravenese (2007; Los Angeles, CA: Paramount Pictures); *Dangerous Minds*, dir. John N. Smith (1995; Hollywood, CA: Hollywood Pictures); and *Cool Runnings*, dir. Jon Turteltaub (1993; Burbank, CA: Walt Disney Pictures).

17. *The Soloist*, dir. Joe Wright (2009; Glendale, CA: Dreamworks, 2009), DVD.

18. Ibid.

19. Ibid.

20. Ibid.

21. Ibid.

22. Hayes and Black, "Troubling Signs."

23. Ibid.

24. Ibid.

25. Ibid.

FIVE

Institutionalization and Gaslighting in *Girl, Interrupted* and *12 Monkeys*

The representation of authoritarian, institutional, gendered, and governmental powers operate as common thematic motifs in texts about people with a mental disorder. Film characters marked as having a mental disorder often appear as frightening and dangerous. According to Stout, Villegas, and Jennings's article "Images of Mental Illness in the Media: Identifying Gaps in the Research," which examines the findings of multiple research studies on the representation of mental disorder, states, "The two outstanding conclusions of media portrayals of persons with mental illness are that they are associated with violence and that they are dangerous and should be avoided."[1] In Hollywood film, people with a mental disorder frequently appear like the criminals in *Psycho* or *The Silence of the Lambs*.[2] People with a mental disorder commonly operate on film as threats against the cinematic common man or woman. They embody the frightening uncertainty of the unknown and the apprehension about random acts of violence from strangers or terrorists. However, the 1995 film *12 Monkeys*, directed by Terry Gilliam; and the 1999 film *Girl, Interrupted*, directed by James Mangold, turn this anxiety from the patient to the fear of authoritarian powers and their ability to gaslight individuals.[3]

The term gaslighting comes from the film *Gaslight* in which Gregory Anton (Charles Boyer) begins to make Ingrid Bergman's character, Paula, think that she is going insane.[4] In her article "Turning up the Lights on Gaslighting," Kate Abramson discusses the origins of the term gaslight and its implementation:

> Very roughly, the phenomenon that's come to be picked out with that term is a form of emotional manipulation in which the gaslighter tries (consciously or not) to induce in someone the sense that her reactions, perceptions, memories and/or beliefs are not just mistaken, but utterly

without grounds—paradigmatically, so unfounded as to qualify as crazy.[5]

This means of manipulation functions both intentionally and accidentally, but cultural or social manipulation that leads to paranoia functions in many films, as the film can be formed to make the audience question the narrator and their own perceptions.

12 Monkeys and *Girl, Interrupted* raise issues of whether the diagnoses of mental disorder justifiably protect the innocent or abusively manipulate vulnerable persons. When the audience sees from the perspective of the characters with a mental disorder, the controlling authority figures become suspicious antagonists. Those in authority physically and emotionally restrain these characters with a mental disorder under the guise of protection and safety from contagion; however, since the main character's perspective dictates the spectator's point of view, the films imbue the narrators with the authority to determine the truth for the audience. Mental disorder is a cinematic gambit to raise epistemological questions of characters' access to knowledge, comprehension of the world, and the importance of who controls society's understanding of truth.

This is especially pertinent in the context of cinema that sometimes features the insane or the paranoid as correct in their assertions about extreme circumstances. They foreshadow catastrophes and frequently make their paranoia appear useful. In films like *Conspiracy Theory* with Mel Gibson, or with the paranoid pilot, Russell Casse, played by Randy Quaid in *Independence Day*, these characters sometimes serve as whistleblowers or literal conspiracy theorists.[6] Their theories seem crazy until they become harbingers of truth.

In *12 Monkeys* and *Girl, Interrupted*, those in authority largely determine reality for characters by punishing outliers, including people with a mental disorder, yet by showing this to the audience, the authority is undermined for the audience. Ironically though, the films do not raise the film industry as an authority that both controls reality and our perceptions of it, because, for example, as we see in *Girl, Interrupted*, the representations of women and sexuality remain controlled by more conventional Hollywood expectations despite the books' more radical perspective.

The control over people with mental disorder has fluctuated over the centuries, and understanding, diagnoses, and standards of care have evolved. In Michel Foucault's book *Discipline and Punish*, he examines the Western power structures internally and externally used to exercise influence over people considered dangerous.[7] His examples begin with medieval villages under the threat of the plague as he walks readers through the physical manifestations of power in varied social and psychological situations. While his description predominantly informs deliberate approaches to punish criminals, it becomes apparent how these techniques have influenced many aspects of modern Western culture. Foucault shows how the bodies of everyone in society become subject to both the mechanisms of control and the impetus that has led to control. In these films, authority figures enact these mechanisms described by Foucault upon characters with a mental disorder as a method of controlling the "contagion" of mental disorder or what is seen here as an illness and to reflect a larger scope of control over anyone who does not conform to their societal expectations. The book shows people with mental disorders as vulnerable to control and often subject to abuses of power.

This control, as described by Foucault, functions as a part of the epistemological question of access to understanding the world. The creators of these films use mental disorder to raise theoretical doubts about the treatment of citizens and their rights. If those in authority claim that a person is crazy or incompetent, then authorities can implement the nearly absolute paternalistic control that appears in *Girl, Interrupted* and *12 Monkeys*. By giving the audience into the perspective of those who have a mental disorder, the audience sees the characters' doubt about authority rather than the authority's version of the truth. This positioning similarly occurs in *Gothika* and *One Flew over the Cuckoo's Nest* where it is not clear who is crazy and who has the right to decide this fact for others.[8] These doubts become significant as the authority figures communicate a different truth than the person with a mental disorder perceives. Foucault's discussion of how power shapes knowledge and understanding becomes noteworthy as the films show how this power can manipulate these characters' perceptions of truth and reality. Their vulnerabilities make the person with a mental disorder doubt reality and the audience doubt the character's honesty in ways that magnify these problematic representations.

Girl, Interrupted depicts Susanna Kaysen's memoir of a year in her life in the 1960s. Susanna, as performed by Winona Ryder, is a young writer who has just graduated high school. The audience learns from the beginning of the film that she has attempted to kill herself with an overdose of aspirin and alcohol. For clarity, and with an understanding of the film's creative license with Kaysen's memoir, I will refer to the author as Kaysen and the character as Susanna. Susanna's parents encourage a Dr. Crumble, as played by Kurtwood Smith, to talk to Susanna. He identifies himself as a friend of the family and a therapist who no longer practices. Dr. Crumble persuades her to admit herself to a mental hospital where the doctors on staff diagnose her with borderline personality disorder. According to the *Diagnostic and Statistical Manual of Mental Disorders: Fifth Edition* (*DSM-5*), symptoms of borderline personality disorder include, but are not limited to, "a pattern of unstable and intense interpersonal relationships . . . impulsivity . . . suicidal behavior . . . [and] difficulty controlling anger."[9] A predominance of the film depicts Susanna's time in the mental hospital. This story line includes intermittent flashbacks to her life prior to the apparent suicide attempt, but the film also punctuates Susanna's experience in the hospital with the predicaments of the other patients and her escape, which ultimately leads to the death of a recently released patient. This dramatic crisis is a turning point in the film where Susanna begins to seek help from the doctors and begins to embrace their therapeutic techniques. The most predominant forms of therapy shown include pharmaceutical options, journaling, and talk therapy or counseling.

As part of the film's ability to question then reaffirm authority, *Girl, Interrupted*'s narrative clearly rests on the audience's engagement with Susanna. The cinematography establishes Susanna from the very first scenes as the primary focus of the camera, both in terms of close-ups and in matches to her eye-line. The audience hears her reflective and seemingly wiser voice from the future as the voice-over frames the film's narrative and echoes the original text of the book. As with the book, the audience experiences her perspective concerning her skepticism about Dr. Crumble's diagnosis.

Throughout most of the film, Susanna questions her own sanity. As narrator, her first monologue begins, "Have you ever confused a dream with life, or stolen something when you have the cash? Have you ever been blue or thought your train moving while sitting still? Maybe I was just crazy, maybe it was just the sixties, or maybe I was just a girl interrupted." This voice-over echoes the book and establishes an initial ambiguity about Susanna's "craziness." The monologue implies that we all have moments of craziness, and Susanna's uncertainty creates doubt about how doctors defined, diagnosed, and evaluated "craziness." This demonstrates her uncertainty about her doctor's diagnosis and undermines the audience's view of the doctor's authority. Later in the narrative, Susanna more explicitly doubts the doctor's diagnosis and looks for a definition of her borderline personality disorder. She looks in a book, presumably the *DSM*, and she reads the book's definition of her disorder. Thus the film encourages the audience to question the doctors' understanding of Susanna's condition and therefore her diagnosis. The structure of the film undermines the doctors' authority, and the film thus creates a space for the audience to wonder at both the doctors' authority and apparent egotistic self-righteousness.

Like Susanna, Jack Nicholson's character, Randle McMurphy, operates in *One Flew over the Cuckoo's Nest* as an example of a narrative that positions the narrator as questionably sane.[10] The institution around McMurphy treats him as a mental patient, but in its portrayal of McMurphy, the film creates doubt about the institution more than the person in question.

After *Girl, Interrupted* initially undermines the authority of the doctors, another level of unreliability applied to the authority figures plays upon the gap between the date of the events shown in the 1960s and the release of the film in 1999. The film presents female patients' sexuality as symptomatic of their mental conditions. By implying that all sexuality by women is a symptom of mental disorder, the film represents an antiquated if traditionally heteronormative and patriarchal understanding of women's sexuality.

Angelina Jolie's character, Lisa, is an interesting counterpoint to Susanna's ambivalence and insecurity. At one point in the film, Susanna asserts, "I don't care," and Lisa returns angrily, "I do care."[11] This seemingly irrelevant exchange illustrates their relationship throughout most of the film. Unlike Susanna, Lisa overtly expresses her sexuality. She frequently uses the word "fuck" for emphasis and punctuation. She also refers to therapy as "the-rape-me." When Susanna reads the definition of her own diagnosis of borderline personality disorder, as she arrives at the list of symptoms including promiscuity, Lisa states, "I like that." Lisa also has an innuendo-filled conversation with an ice-cream server, which leads to fits of giggling by the other patients. Later, Lisa facilitates Susanna's sexual encounter with her visiting boyfriend by stalling the orderly. During Lisa and Susanna's final escape, hinting at a homosexual attraction, they kiss. The film presents all these markers of sexuality as apparently deviant and indicators of illness rather than typical human sexuality. This both dates the events in the film, as firmly entrenched in the medical diagnostic eras of the past, because the earlier versions of the *DSM* listed homosexuality as a mental disorder. Unfortunately, in addition to that, the 1999 film does not, in contrast with the critically aware book, do much to dissuade the audience of women's sexuality being inappropriate or deviant.

Lisa is a tragic figure in the film, doomed to her illness indefinitely and becomes the contrasting tale and the narrative's rebel, which shows Susanna how not to behave. Lisa's influence especially leads Susanna down the perilous road to rebellion, including to the homosexual kiss, the death of Daisy (Brittany Murphy), and the breaking of numerous hospital rules. Lisa is a femme fatale figure who rather than drawing a male protagonist to his doom, functions as a charismatic sexual seductress who lures all of the women around her toward dangerous behavior. The film follows classic Hollywood tradition by condemning an aggressively sexual woman and by pathologizing sexuality. Thus the doctors create a space where the women feel broken because the doctors invalidate their emotions and perceptions. The audience sees this invalidation of the women, but the film does not seem to problematize it in the ways that the book criticized overtly.

Girl, Interrupted connects Lisa's sexuality and female sexuality in general to mental disorder. The definition of borderline personality disorder, as read by Susanna, includes promiscuity; and Lisa's constant innuendo reinforces this notion that sexuality in women operates as an indicator of mental disorder. When the women are reading each other's diagnoses,

Lisa calls Jillian Armenante's character, Cynthia, a "dyke" as a diagnosis. The film implies that the doctors considered homosexuality a disorder, which would have been common as the *DSM* listed homosexuality as a psychological disorder. By locating female sexuality as crazy, the film reaffirms the patriarchal social conventions that reject female sexuality as natural. Especially by marking sexuality between women as wrong, Lisa becomes the exemplar of this sexuality as crazy and inappropriate, apparently influencing Susanna, as Susanna initiates the kiss with Lisa.

By making female sexuality symptomatic of mental disorder rather than natural, the film reinforces classic Hollywood traditions of condemning sexual female characters, especially the aforementioned femme fatale, or a dangerous woman who through being sexually authoritative destroys others, usually the male protagonist. Patriarchal authority and control, contain and limit Lisa and Susanna, especially in the film.

Susanna's sexuality is a symptom of her disorder. Even the relationship with her English teacher becomes a symptom of borderline personality disorder, rather than the predatory act of an authority figure. In her article "Borderline Girlhoods: Mental Illness, Adolescence, and Femininity in *Girl, Interrupted*," Elizabeth Marshall argues,

> The doctors at McLean gloss over the teacher's power in relation to his female student, or the possibility of Kaysen's desire for him. They define it as an "attachment" (Kaysen 85). It is not the English teacher who lacks boundaries. Rather, it is Kaysen, who is diagnosed as lacking healthy boundaries. Kaysen's personality is so ill-defined that she cannot distinguish between healthy attachments and unhealthy ones, and she takes the blame.[12]

The film asserts that Susanna's sexuality is, like her illness, her own responsibility and seemingly wrong. Marshall also notes that the title of the book and ultimately the film implies otherwise, as it alludes to a painting by Vermeer titled *Girl Interrupted at Her Music*. In this painting, an older man looms over a young woman. This image of an "interrupted" girl establishes that the interruption begins externally. The film's voiceover implies that the interruption was the illness and that when she decided to overcome it, it went away. In contrast, the title's allusion implies that the English teacher instigated the interruption in her life. In this and other instances, the rejection of authority in the book becomes diluted in the cinematic telling of this memoir. In the less progressive film, Susanna causes her own problems, while the book places blame on the predatory English teacher. Again, the initial critique of authority falls to passivity and acceptance of rules which, in the film, accommodates a happy ending which the disillusionment in the book does not provide.

The film also undermines the apparent authority through Susanna's diagnoses as it becomes clear that anyone who does not fit into the college-bound, well-behaved, socially acceptable adolescent categories becomes diagnosable. Yet while the film establishes these motifs of disenfranchised youth being committed, it slowly shows acceptance of some diagnoses. Unlike the film, Kaysen's book does not accept the authority's seeming righteousness but continues to refute it. The film shifts its suspicion from the doctors to Lisa and seems to accept the borderline personality disorder and the therapeutic solution of talk therapy. In the film, conforming mentally by accepting the diagnosed disorder, journaling about herself and her fellow patients, and ostensibly following the hospital rules gets Susanna released from the institution. In contrast, in the book, marriage and conforming physically to the feminine ideal allow her to go home. The book has a more consistent feminist agenda in its examination of the societal influences; at the same time, the film concedes that if Susanna just desires to get better she will succeed. In "Borderline Girlhoods," Marshall argues:

> Throughout the memoir, Kaysen makes visible how the gendered pedagogies frame her diagnosis and treatment. However, the pedagogies Kaysen counters are recuperated in the movie. Numerous differences exist between the film and the memoir . . . the film re-asserts the adolescent girl as a "hyper-sensitive" subject, who paradoxically is empowered through her vulnerability.[13]

The film's initial move to challenge authority ultimately fails in a markedly unsatisfying way that dangerously asserts mental disorder as the lazy way out for people who do not want to take responsibility for their own actions. Despite the film's failure to consistently challenge the narrative of blaming the patient for her illness, it does show the manipulative and risky tools of the doctors.

The questionable authority figures throughout the film use their positions to control the incarcerated women in a variety of ways. Many of these operate clearly under Foucault's paradigm of the panopticon. Foucault states, "He who is subjected to a field of visibility, and who knows it, assumes responsibility for the constraints of power; he makes them play spontaneously upon himself; he inscribes in himself the power relation which he simultaneously plays both roles; he becomes the principle of his own subjection."[14] The panopticon is a literal or figurative structure of control like a prison, a guard, or a camera that makes a person feel constantly watched, therefore leading the person to behave as if they are actually being watched.

After Susanna has entered the hospital, the nurse Valerie, played by Whoopi Goldberg, gives her the tour of the hospital where she informs Susanna that the nurses will limit a patient's movements and communication. At the end of the tour, a nurse enters Susanna's new room and says "checks."[15] These checks occur every fifteen minutes for the women and periodically throughout the movie. The nurses consistently enter the patients' rooms despite small glass windows into each. The hospital does not even afford women the illusion of privacy in order to constantly reinforce the power and control of the staff.

The film reiterates this control in the scene where Susanna wants to shave her legs. She sits in a bathtub as Nurse Valerie watches her shave. This supervision occurs ostensibly so that she does not attempt suicide with the blade. The hospital workers watch the patients constantly, either in their physical intrusion of the rooms or from their glass box positioned at the center of the hall, reminiscent of Foucault's proposed prison in which a guard sits central to the prisoners' cells so they are always being surveilled. The patients learn to internalize the feeling of being watched. Susanna's roommate, Georgiana, played by Clea DuVall, tells Susanna, "They'll space them out after you've been here awhile."[16] Once the patients have proven themselves submissive to the institutional rules or have internalized their constant supervision and become docile, they need less external supervision.

The film shows the internalization of the patriarchal authority and implies that Susanna's mental disorder appeared as a symptom of her resistance to accept society's rules for her. Nurse Valerie and Doctor Wick (Vanessa Redgrave) tell Susanna that she must help herself in order to recover. As the film begins, doctors convince Susanna to sign herself in. While she physically signs the commitment papers, the authority figures exert pressure on her to do so. During various sessions with Susanna, the doctors and nurses write about Susanna on notepads and on prescriptive sheets. It is in these notes that Susanna finds the diagnosis of borderline personality disorder. The transition in the film toward Susanna's "cure" starts as she begins to write more intensively about herself. She must use the writing to explore her issues and to accept the problems that doctors diagnosed her with. She must not only read what the psychologists wrote about her, but she must write down these diagnoses in her own words to become cured. This internalization and acceptance of the authority around her shows how the doctors have come to control her. She becomes her own watcher. She internalizes their scrutiny and applies it to herself enough that the doctors consider her well and ready to leave.

The two authority figures who most convincingly persuade Susanna to accept the dictates and treatments of the hospital are Dr. Wick and Nurse Valerie. Despite being a woman, Dr. Wick exhibits a notably masculine affect and position in the film, even being called "Dr. Dyke." Her attitude and authority position her at a distance from Susanna and reaffirm her role as the face of the authoritarian institution. Nurse Valerie is a more supportive figure, but both women communicate to Susanna the same advice. Dr. Wick and Nurse Valerie both tell Susanna that she is responsible for her own mental disorder. Valerie tells her, "You're a lazy, self-indulgent little girl who's driving herself crazy."[17] *Girl, Interrupted* affirms the questionable and possibly dangerous advice that willpower alone can overcome a mental disorder. Susanna's roommate, Georgiana, refers to *The Wizard of Oz* several times, implying that to extract herself from mental disorder she must believe that she can recover to go home. The happy endings in *The Wizard of Oz* and *Girl, Interrupted* are part of the larger pattern of classic Hollywood resolutions that reinforce the status quo and bring the characters home either literally or figuratively back into the fold of their family and expected societal roles. Despite the feminist undertones of a story about women evolving together and Susanna's initial resistance, this is a reaffirmation of the patriarchal psychological perspective and a demonstration of the internalization of the power and discipline being heaped upon patients.

In contrast, the memoir communicates a different message that does not reinforce the idea that talk therapy solves Susanna's problems but resists the repeated narrative of girlhood instability. Marshall describes the book's oppositional and revolutionary approach: "The withdrawn and silent heroine, guided by a well-adjusted adult, reaches a therapeutic breakthrough that allows her to speak about and recover from her past trauma. Kaysen has no such eureka moment."[18] While the book argues that societal conditions led Susanna to her attempted suicide and subsequent institutionalization, the film affirms those institutional and societal powers as right in their judgment of Susanna and the solution to her problems. The film initially hints at defiance but ultimately reaffirms submission to power, as Susanna becomes "cured" when she rejects the defiant sexual Lisa and commits to talk therapy with Dr. Wick.

Because the audience looks through Susanna's perspective, they are encouraged to doubt or accept power and their truths when she does. The audience's first impression of the psychological profession comes from Susanna's initial discussion with a highly suspicious Dr. Crumble. In one of the film's first scenes, Susanna speaks to Dr. Crumble, who is an academic psychologist and her father's colleague. She describes her perception of the events surrounding an apparent suicide attempt. The doctor states that she "chased a bottle of aspirin with a bottle of vodka" as evidence that she attempted to kill herself.[19] She unconvincingly retorts that she had a headache. This denial both undermines her view of the seriousness of her action and alters his perception that she intended to commit suicide. She does not seem reliable here, but her resistance to his explanation establishes her doubt and also his paternalistic attitude. "Susanna, your father is a friend of mine. He is a colleague. He asked me to see you, even though I don't do this anymore. You're hurting everyone around you."[20] Ostensibly, Dr. Crumble sends Susanna away, not because she needs help, but rather because her continued presence inconveniences everyone else. This makes Dr. Crumble and Susanna's family seem selfish and her commitment to a mental hospital seem suspicious and overzealous. It is emblematic of Foucault's description of the way that people with a mental disorder have been locked away for numerous reasons, often due to the fear and anxiety of the culture rather than for the good of the individual with a mental disorder.[21]

To reinforce the audience's suspicion of his authority, Dr. Crumble's book *The Inner Working of the Mind* sits on the coffee table, and as he turns away, Susanna reads the dust jacket. With her reaction and his tone, it establishes him as pompous and self-important rather than caring or supportive. He appears as a distant academic who does not practice, yet he will quickly commit Susanna for her parents' convenience. He tells her that she needs to go to the mental hospital and talks about it being "restful" and "easier" for her parents. As part of the film's ability to question then reaffirm authority, Susanna's perspective of the initially questionable presentation of psychology and authority creates doubt about the validity of her being sent away. Suspicion of Dr. Crumble's dubious authority becomes part of the narrative's exploration of power and control over Susanna's truth about herself.

Susanna's parents use Dr. Crumble to dispel their authority. The camera only shows Susanna's mother at a distance outside the home and later in her car as the taxi driver takes Susanna away. These long shots establish an emotional distance for the mother while the audience never sees the father. The parents defer their responsibility to others, in particular, Dr. Crumble. This indicates that their decision serves their own inability to parent and confront Susanna's issues, rather than her need to be institutionalized. They want others to deal with their problem child, in the same way that Susanna does not want to deal with her own problems. The adults all eschew the responsibility for Susanna's issues. Susanna may indeed be in need of institutionalization, but the cinematic representation delivers her critical perspective on the idea that her parents or Dr. Crumble have her best interests in mind. This initial, if subtle, undermining of the psychological field and authority figures, in general, undermines the diagnosis and lessons later. This changes by the end of the film, when Susanna comes to believe the doctors about their perception of her that includes her need for help.

Susanna's doubts about authority and her understanding of her mental disorder raise the audience's suspicions about the legitimacy of the character's hospitalization, despite her suicide attempt. The doctor's resultant use of supervision and the women's internalization of control in order to manage them creates a space for the audience to also be suspicious of the doctors, their diagnoses, and their understanding of Susanna's truth—that is, until the end of the film that, unlike the book, settles into the patriarchal and condescending reaffirmation of Susanna's problems being her own fault and solvable with grit and effort.

Susanna's narrative is a prescriptive tale that ostensibly shares the story of self-affirmation and self-control but unfortunately places the blame of mental disorder on the person experiencing it while reaffirming the patriarchal sexual politics of the past. The more consistently critical memoir highlights how the film conforms to the fatalistic end for the femme fatale and the Hollywood imperative for a happy ending, whereas the book effectively claims that the idea of home was also an illusion. In contrast, the film has Susanna go home apparently happy well behaved and no longer disillusioned by her journey of momentary defiance. She succumbs to the belief that she was crazy and that only she could make herself better. *12 Monkeys* inverts this narrative by telling the story of a man who must believe he is not crazy to succeed.

The 1995 film *12 Monkeys*, directed by Terry Gilliam and starring Bruce Willis, Madeleine Stowe, and Brad Pitt, tells the story of a convict who traveled back in time to 1996 to uncover the source of a virus that killed most of the Earth's population. *12 Monkeys* was inspired by a 1962 French short film, *La Jetée,* which included a similar if much more basic narrative of time travel.[22] *12 Monkeys* begins by following James Cole (Bruce Willis) and his subsequent forcible commitment to an asylum. The psychiatrist and love interest, Kathryn Railly (Madeleine Stowe), lives in what I will refer to as the film's present: 1990 and then 1996. This is Dr. Railly's present and occurs approximately on the date of the film's release. Two parallel narratives operate together in the film. The primary mystery explores the origin of the apocalyptic virus. Cole's mental institutionalization establishes the film's secondary mystery of whether or not the postapocalyptic future is real or a figment of Cole's psychotic imagination.

The film establishes doubt of Cole and the audience's perceptions from the first moment. The title card appears as the first image in *12 Monkeys.* It reads, "5 billion people will die from a deadly virus in 1997 . . . The Survivors will abandon the surface of the planet . . . once again the animals will rule the world. . ."[23] The sound of a typewriter echoes as these words are then followed by the lines "Excerpts from interview with clinically diagnosed paranoid schizophrenic, April 12, 1990—Baltimore County Hospital."[24] This information and then its source undermine the previous lines' reliability, and they immediately raise the issue of the believability of Cole's point of view. This cinematic gambit creates uncertainty about the film's truth and whether the audience has access to it. The camera and ultimately the film itself operate as a layer of authority, both giving and denying us access to the truth of the narrative. By making the film's imagery dubious, it imbues all layers of truth around it with suspicion. The audience comes to not only understand that the lead James Cole may be unreliable, but anything that the text provides may be less than credible.

The film shows the primary authority figures dictating the lives of Cole and other inmates. The powerful figures in the future appear as scientists who use inmates to accomplish dangerous tasks by going above ground in the virus-laden environment. Their dictatorial and manipulative behavior reflects a frighteningly oppressive level of control in the vein of fascist regimes or other cautionary futuristic science fiction. The scientists willingly sacrifice Cole for the greater good of the community, with only his nominal assent. Both the future scientists and the present's psychologists appear in long shots where they sit in a long row and judge Cole's fitness for their literal or physical prescriptions. The parallel representations of the psychologists of the present confine and restrain Cole, ostensibly for his own protection. Through the lack of sympathy, the similar imagery to the future scientists, and the parallel conditions of Cole's involuntary commitment, the film implies that the psychologists are primarily concerned with their own protection. These suspicious figures in the future and the present create an atmosphere of doubt about authority and its right to control people, even for ostensibly benevolent reasons like curing disease.

In *12 Monkeys* the recurring theme of contagion and disease raises the level of paranoia in the text and also establishes the narrative's tension about the truth of Cole's reliability and ultimately his sanity. Some of the first scenes of Cole in the future world infected with the mysterious virus show him dressing in a large plastic suit to go outside and find animal or insect specimens to test. The film's imagery repeats this plastic covering in the clear plastic raincoat he wears the first time that he travels to the present. Cole's first choice in the virus-free world of 1990 shows his need to protect himself. It then becomes obvious with his commitment to a mental institution that the police, psychologists, and orderlies believe that Cole represents a threat. The film deliberately plays with our ability to trust Cole by alternately making him look ludicrous as he drools and rocks under medication, then showing the audience the future world in elaborate detail to reaffirm its existence.

This level of control in *12 Monkeys* illustrates the structure of power discussed by Foucault in *Discipline and Punish*. This fear of disease and infection is one of the earliest rationales for the kinds of disciplines he describes in the chapter titled "Panopticism."[25] Foucault describes a medieval town dealing with the plague by isolating the villagers in their homes and limiting their access to other people. The isolation of those considered dangerous instigates the various measures of control that Foucault describes. The film represents these fears throughout and shows the institutions in control attempting to confine and limit the normates' exposure to disease or perceived mental disorder.[26]

One of the film's most explicit examples of containment is explained by Jeffrey Goines (Brad Pitt), the psychotic who Cole meets in the asylum. Goines expounds to Cole on the subject of psychological commitment and the patients' access to the outside world: "Telephone call, telephone call, That's communication with the outside world. Doctor's discretion. No. If all of these nuts could just make phone calls, it could spread insanity oozing through the telephone cables, oozing to the ears of all those poor, sane people, infecting them. Wackos everywhere! A plague of madness."[27] This film explicitly compares mental disorder to a disease that must be controlled and contained, thus establishing the binary mentioned by Foucault that he describes as a function of power: "Generally speaking, all the authorities exercising individual control function according to a double mode; that of binary division and branding (mad/sane; dangerous/harmless; normal/abnormal)."[28] Cole is either psychotic or telling the truth. He is either dangerous or sane. The authorities as embodied by the scientists and psychologists in the film ensure that no middle ground exists. The audience's investment in this question of sanity becomes the crux of the film's mystery and frames our understanding of whether we feel sympathy for the abuses being heaped upon Cole or whether we believe that he needs an involuntary commitment. Since these remain the only two options presented to the audience, we become limited by this binary understanding of Cole and the film's reality. We enact the society's judgment of Cole as the film asks us to judge him and the truth for ourselves.

As Foucault describes the panopticon, he explains: "Visibility is a trap."[29] The ability of supervisors to oversee "prisoners" is a tool to observe, limit, and influence the actions of others. The scientists and the psychologists who have the power in *12 Monkeys* can see Cole more clearly than Cole can typically see them, but they also make Cole feel watched, regardless of their actual presence. As Foucault describes, even more significant than knowing what the prisoners are doing, the panopticon establishes in people the internalized feeling of always being watched.

Perhaps the most grotesque manifestation of the embodied panopticon appears during Cole's time in the future. The panel of scientists consistently stare at, scrutinize, and observe him. In one of the initial scenes of Cole's interviews with the scientists, they ask him to sit down in a chair that abruptly raises up on the wall. He effectively becomes trapped on the wall, reminiscent of a bug being pinned to an entomologist's display board. The scientists stare at him from a safe distance while the film shows their views moderated by goggles or glasses. They also look at him through a large spherical contraption covered in small screens which all show the scientists' eyes. The screened contraption's design intimidates Cole as the scientists use it to look at him and make sure that he knows about their exaggerated mechanical gaze. The screens showing scientists' eyes ensure that Cole and the film's audience know that they watch him. This device approaches him jerkily and invades his personal space like a doctor examining a patient, but the actual scientists are able to remain at a safe distance from Cole. Their looking appears conspicuous on the cinematic screen. As Foucault describes the individual being confined, "He is seen, but he does not see; he is the object of information, never a subject in communication."[30] While Cole can see the scientists on a limited basis, the mechanical obstructions between them increase their view and obscure his. Foucault states that the panopticon "is an important mechanism, for it automatizes and disindividualizes power."[31] This impression of being watched becomes internalized as Cole begins to see the people in the street that he presumes are agents from the future.

Figure 5.1. James Cole is closely observed by this spherical eye-like device. It is covered in screens that show the scientists looking at Cole. Terry Gilliam's 1995 *12 Monkeys*.

Cole frequently obverses strangers in the film's present watching him. Despite the fact that Cole's rather erratic behavior is adequate justification for askance looks from any typical passerby, Cole takes these reactions as indicators that the future scientists' underlings constantly follow him. The film provides no evidence that most of these people come from the future, and the audience easily concludes that some or perhaps many of these figures operate only as objects of Cole's paranoia rather than actual spies from the future. The future scientists succeed at creating what Foucault calls the "major effect of the Panopticon: to induce in the inmate a state of conscious and permanent visibility that assures the automatic functioning of power."[32] Whether he is being watched becomes insignificant, because he believes he is being watched and will ultimately behave accordingly. This can be seen in many other films with characters with mental disorder. *Fight Club* illustrates some of these same signals of paranoia. Similarly, Mel Gibson in *Conspiracy Theory*, and Russell Crowe's John Nash in *A Beautiful Mind* operate as paranoid characters whose narratives play with whether the character is crazy or right. Cole, Susanna in *Girl, Interrupted*, and these other characters become so fearful of being watched that they always act as if watched and become a tool of their own control.

Later in the film, at the height of Cole's paranoia, he pulls out some of his own teeth because he believes they contain tracking devices. He emerges from a hotel bathroom with blood dripping down his face and shirt. His teeth are in his hands. This both appears as a moment of probable psychosis and an indicator that he has become convinced that the scientists from the future are following him. If he is correct, then his actions are somewhat reasonable in an effort to escape their pursuit. If he is merely paranoid, then this moment of self-mutilation functions at the height of his psychotic break. The future scientists have literally gotten into Cole's head. It is unclear to the audience if this is ultimately true, which places us in Cole's position. The film *Gothika* also plays on the main character's inability to be sure if she is crazy or sane. The narrative ends up a ghost story, but the institutional control of her sanity and her perspective position the audience in a similar place of uncertainty about what in the film is real and how we as an audience might know that.

12 Monkeys features crazy characters and a potentially crazy central consciousness to make the audience wonder who can see the truth and if they even have access to the film's truth. This challenges assumptions about reality. The scientists make Cole doubt his own perceptions, and if he cannot believe himself, then he cannot trust anyone. This film asks the audience to question our own perceptions through Cole and presumably look reflectively about our own perceptions of reality and authority.

Both *Girl, Interrupted* and *12 Monkeys* operate around questions of sanity. If the central characters are insane, then the films imply that the authority figures in the form of scientists and psychologists justifiably confine and manipulate their charges. However, if Susanna and Cole are sane, then the behavior of those in power becomes abusive, manipulative, and dangerous. Perhaps the scariest element of the two films is the way that institutional powers can influence the beliefs of the subjects about their own sanity. If others, especially those in power, determine another person's sanity, then they also control freedom. Both films raise issues of who determines the truth surrounding the lead characters, and neither film leaves the truth within the power of the individual. The films critique authoritarian control through their ability to achieve absolute authority over these individuals and ultimately their access to truth.

NOTES

1. Patricia A. Stout, Jorge Villegas, and Nancy A. Jennings, "Images of Mental Illness in the Media: Identifying Gaps in the Research," *Schizophrenia Bulletin* 30 (2004): 558.
2. *Psycho,* dir. Alfred Hitchcock (1960; Universal City, CA: Shamley Productions, 2012), DVD; and *The Silence of the Lambs,* dir. Jonathan Demme (1991; Santa Monica, CA: Strong Heart/ Demme Production, 2007), DVD.
3. *12 Monkeys,* dir. Terry Gilliam (1995; Universal City, CA: Universal Pictures, 2005), DVD.
4. *Gaslight,* dir. George Cukor (1938; Beverly Hills, CA: Metro-Goldwyn-Mayer).
5. Kate Abramson, 2014. "Turning up the Lights on Gaslighting." *Nous-Supplement: Philosophical Perspectives* 28, 1–30.

6. *Conspiracy Theory*, dir. Richard Donner (1997; Burbank, CA: Warner Brothers); and *Independence Day*, dir. Roland Emmerich (1996; Los Angeles, CA: Twentieth Century Fox).

7. Michel Foucault. *Discipline and Punish: The Birth of the Prison* (New York: Pantheon Books, 1977).

8. *Gothika*, dir. Mathieu Kassovitz (2003; Culver City, CA: Columbia Pictures Corporation); and *One Flew over the Cuckoo's Nest*, dir. Miloš Forman (1975; Berkeley, CA: Fantasy Films).

9. *DSM-5*, 663.

10. *One Flew over the Cuckoo's Nest*.

11. *Girl, Interrupted*, dir. James Mangold (1999; Culver City, CA: Sony Pictures, 2000), DVD.

12. Elizabeth Marshall, "Borderline Girlhoods: Mental Illness, Adolescence, and Femininity in *Girl, Interrupted*," *The Lion And The Unicorn*, no. 1 (2006): 117.

13. Ibid.

14. Michel Foucault. *Discipline and Punish: The Birth of the Prison* (New York: Random House, 1995), 202–203.

15. *Girl, Interrupted*.

16. *Girl, Interrupted*.

17. Ibid.

18. Marshall, "Borderline Girlhoods," 125.

19. *Girl, Interrupted*.

20. Ibid.

21. Michel Foucault, *Madness and Civilization: A History of Insanity in the Age of Reason* (New York: Vintage Books, 1995), 199–201.

22. *La Jetée*, dir. Chris Marker (1962; France: Argo Films).

23. *12 Monkeys*.

24. Ibid.

25. Foucault, *Discipline and Punish*, 195.

26. Ibid., 195.

27. *12 Monkeys*.

28. Foucault, *Discipline and Punish*, 199.

29. Ibid., 200.

30. Ibid.

31. Ibid., 202.

32. Ibid., 201.

Conclusion

This book engages in the convergence of representations of mental disorder with the ways that Hollywood's limited depictions shape its own limited truth. Each individual chapter works to uncover different approaches to control and their intersection with other forms of oppression. While this book does not discuss the real-life consequences of skewed, pitying, or inaccurate representations, one can see in examples like *Rain Man*'s influence on public awareness of autism spectrum disorder, and how cinematic portrayals shape our cultural consciousness about a subject. These consequences make representations important.

The lengths of movies, varieties of bodies shown, and the types of violence allowed on network television can become rote until they change and then they feel disruptive. In a course on American literature, I frequently teach Kate Chopin's short story "The Storm." During this brief narrative, the lead characters have an affair. After cheating, the characters return to their respective spouses, and the final line of the work reads, "So the storm passed and everyone was happy."[1] This last line has a tendency to frustrate some of my students. They commonly insist that there must be problems later in the marriage, or that something must go wrong as a consequence of the characters' infidelity. This argument comes in stark contrast to the text, which clearly asserts that the characters live happily ever after. These are also fictional characters, so to insist that there be events contrary to the narrative shows the students' strong feeling that the bad be punished and the narrative put to rights. These students, like most of us, exist in a deluge of classic or popular Hollywood films, Disney cartoons, and network television that punishes the sinful, rewards the virtuous, and commonly follows capitalistic American Anglo-Saxon Christian/Judeo ethics. I teach "The Storm" in part to discuss how contrived and unlike reality this expectation really is. We live in a world where people who do bad things sometimes escape prosecution and where good people sometimes go to prison. However, the prevalence of these strict narrative rules in the students' dominant forms of media becomes evident and disruptive when stories break these rules. The students resist the sinful characters not experiencing punishment, because it frustrates decades of narrative reinforcement.

The example of "The Storm" illustrates my point about spectator expectations because of its overt sin and clearly happy ending. While people with disabilities in film do not necessarily sin, they frequently break the kinds of social conventions that a film cannot neatly resolve happily in 120 minutes. Mental disorder does not have an easy answer. This often leaves punishment or control as the only clear resolution for these complex characters, unless the narrative can contain them in other ways, for example, like the "structure of pity" described in the chapter on *Radio* and *The Soloist*.

While there are exceptions in Hollywood to the rules that dictate the fate of femmes fatales and African Americans with disabilities, the social imperative for film to reinforce, confirm, and maintain its hierarchies is profound. Too commonly the Other in the form of minorities, people with physical disabilities, people with mental disorders, women, or other cultural outliers endure the repetitive depiction of disenfranchising portrayals. This may come in the form of exceptionalism, pity, or oppression. With more awareness of the marginalization of those who are not wealthy white cis gendered normate men, through efforts like #oscarsowhite or #metoo, I hope that films will move toward, not just more representations of Others but also better representations of Others.

Works like *Mozart and the Whale, Adam,* or *Silver Linings Playbook* provide examples of works that move toward engagement of primary characters with mental disorders. These films do not reflect as much of the typical pity as many representations and thus break some of the boundaries outlined in this book. In *Mozart and the Whale,* the two romantic leads are both identified as being on the autistic spectrum. These elements serve to recommend this movie as an exemplar of representations. However, it accomplishes these goals by depicting relatively mild conditions. Also, this film in its primary narration still depicts financially stable, white, heteronormative, attractive figures who engage in a classic Hollywood romance that travels from the meet-cute to the marriage-like ending. It demonstrates momentum in the movement toward better representation but resists making a radical or essentially meaningful statement and reduces autism to somewhat quirky character traits and heightened anxiety.

Unfortunately, people with mental disorders continue to be frequently portrayed as crazy people that cinema confines, pities, and kills. Even benevolent attempts to depict characters with disabilities frequently reduce their lead characters to pitiable props to demonstrate the growth of others. *Radio*'s moral reinforces that Radio should be treated well because it is good for the "normal" townspeople. Even with a seemingly progressive film about an African American man with schizophrenia like *The Soloist* or men who challenge capitalism in *Fight Club*, the myth of the white savior male ideal of masculinity triumphantly endures. Women, in contrast, suffer at the altar of male ego and frequently die under its weight.

Because people, including myself, first saw a person with autism and learned the meaning of the word autistic by watching *Rain Man*, it becomes evident how powerful these representations are for how these conditions become a part of the cultural consciousness. However, as Hollywood has never operated as a harbinger of truths in entertainment, but rather an opiate of half-truths, the responsibility for depicting a psychological condition well and honestly will never be its first priority. That being said, with advocacy and influences outside of Hollywood, hopefully, the diversity and complexity of engaging powerful characters with mental disorders will become common rather than exceptional.

NOTE

1. Kate Chopin, "The Storm," in *Norton Anthology of American Literature, Eighth Edition,* ed. Nina Baym (New York: W. W. Norton & Company, 2013), 1620.

Bibliography

12 Monkeys, dir. Terry Gilliam. 1995; Universal City, CA: Universal Studios, 2005. DVD.
Abramson, Kate. "Turning up the Lights on Gaslighting." *Nous-Supplement: Philosophical Perspectives* 28 (2014): 1–30.
Adam, dir. Max Mayer, 2009; Century City, CA: Fox Searchlight Pictures.
Afra, Kia. "PG-13, Ratings Creep, and the Legacy of Screen Violence: The MPAA Responds to the FTC's 'Marketing Violent Entertainment to Children' (2000–2009)." *Cinema Journal* 55, no. 3 (2016): 46.
Atypical, 2017; Culver City, CA: Sony Pictures Television.
Batman Begins, dir. Christopher Nolan. 2005; Burbank, CA: Warner Brothers Entertainment.
Beautiful Mind, A, dir. Ron Howard, 2001; Universal City, CA: Universal Pictures.
Beauvoir, Simone de. 1991. *The Second Sex.* London: Vintage Books.
Belcher, Christina, and Kimberly Maich. "Autism Spectrum Disorder in Popular Media: Storied Reflections of Societal Views." *Brock Education: A Journal of Educational Research And Practice* 23, no. 2 (2014): 97–115.
Big Bang Theory, The, 2007–2018; Burbank, CA: Warner Brothers Television.
Birth of a Nation, dir. D. W. Griffith and Thomas Dixon. 1915; Los Angeles, CA: Triangle Film Corp, 2013. DVD.
Black, Gregory D. *Hollywood Censored: Morality Codes, Catholics, and the Movies.* New York: Cambridge University Press, 1994.
Black Swan, dir. Darren Aronofsky. 2011; Beverly Hills, CA: Fox Searchlight Pictures, 2011. DVD.
Bob's Burgers, 2011–2018; North Hollywood, CA: Bento Box Entertainment.
Breaking Bad, dir. Rian Johnson and Vince Gilligan, 2009; Culver City, CA: Sony Pictures Home Entertainment.
Butler, Judith. *Undoing Gender.* New York: Routledge, 2004.
Cabinet of Dr. Caligari, The, dir. Robert Wiene. 1921; Potsdam, Germany, UFA GmbH.
Chopin, Kate. "The Storm," *Norton Anthology of American Literature,* edited by Nina Baym, 1618–20. New York: W. W. Norton & Company, 2013.
Cool Runnings, dir. Jon Turteltaub. 1993; Burbank, CA: Walt Disney Pictures.
Cross, Simon. *Mediating Madness: Mental Distress and Cultural Representation.* London: Palgrave Macmillan, 2010.
Dangerous Minds, dir. John N. Smith. 1995; Hollywood, CA: Hollywood Pictures.
Dark Knight, The, dir. Christopher Nolan, 2008; Burbank, CA: Warner Brothers Entertainment.
Dark Knight Rises, The dir. Christopher Nolan, 2012; Burbank, CA: Warner Brothers Entertainment.
Dexter, dir. James Manos Jr. 2007; Los Angeles, CA: Showtime Entertainment.
Diagnostic and Statistical Manual of Mental Disorders: Fifth Edition. Washington, DC: American Psychiatric Association, 2013.
Elephant Man, The, dir. David Lynch. 1980; Culver City, CA: Brooksfilms, 2001. DVD.
Fight Club, dir. David Fincher. 1999; Beverly Hills, CA: Fox 2000 Pictures, 2000. DVD.
Fisher, Mark, and Amber Jacobs. "Debating Black Swan: Gender and Horror." *Film Quarterly* 65, no. 1 (2011): 58–62.
Foucault, Michel. *Discipline and Punish: The Birth of the Prison.* New York: Vintage Books, 1995.

———. *Madness and Civilization: A History of Insanity in the Age of Reason.* New York: Vintage Books, 1995.
Freedom Writers, dir. Richard LaGravenese. 2007; Los Angeles, CA: Paramount Pictures.
Gatens, Moira. "Power, Bodies and Difference" in *Feminist Theory and the Body: A Reader*, edited by Price, Janet, and Margrit Shildrick, 227-234. New York: Routledge, 1999.
Girl, Interrupted, dir. James Mangold. 1999; Culver City, CA: Sony Pictures, 2000. DVD.
Girl with the Dragon Tattoo, The, dir. David Fincher. 2011; Los Angeles, CA: Scott Rudlin Productions.
Giroux, Henry A., and Imre Szeman. "IKEA Boy and the Politics of Male Bonding: Fight Club, Consumerism, and Violence." *New Art Examiner* 28, no. 4 (December 2000): 32–61.
Good Doctor, The, created by David Shore. 2017–2018; New York: American Broadcasting Company.
Gothika, dir. Mathieu Kassovitz. 2003; Culver City, CA: Columbia Pictures Corporation.
Harper, Stephen. *Madness, Power and the Media: Class, Gender and Race in Popular Representations of Mental Distress.* London: Palgrave Macmillan, 2009.
Hayes, Michael T., and Rhonda S. Black. "Troubling Signs: Disability, Hollywood Movies and the Construction of a Discourse of Pity." *Disability Studies Quarterly* 23, no. 2 (Spring 2003). http://dsq-sds.org/article/view/419/585 (accessed December 5, 2017).
Hughey, Matthew W. "Racializing Redemption, Reproducing Racism: The Odyssey of Magical Negroes and White Saviors." *Sociology Compass* 6, no. 9 (2012): 751–767.
Imitation Game, The, dir. Morten Tyldum. 2015; New York: The Weinstein Company.
Kellner, Douglass. "Poltergeists, Gender, and Class in the Age of Reagan and Bush." In *The Hidden Foundation: Cinema and the Question of Class*, edited by David E. James and Rick Berg, 217–39. Minneapolis: University of Minnesota Press, 1996.
Kondo, Naomi. 2008. "Mental Illness in Film." *Psychiatric Rehabilitation Journal* 31, no. 3: 250–52.
La Jetée, dir. Chris Marker. 1962; France: Argo Films.
Lion in Winter, The, dir. Anthony Harvey. 1968; Santa Monica, CA MGM, 2001. DVD.
Love Actually, dir. Richard Curtis. 2003; Universal City, CA, Universal Pictures, 2003. DVD.
Lukin, Josh. "Disability and Blackness." In *The Disability Studies Reader*, edited by Lennard J. Davis, 308–15. New York: Routledge, 2013.
Man Who Knew Too Much, The, dir. Alfred Hitchcock. 1956; Los Angeles, CA: Paramount Pictures, 2006.
Marsh, Jessecae, and Lindzi Shanks. "Thinking You Can Catch Mental Illness: How Beliefs about Membership Attainment and Category Structure Influence Interactions with Mental Health Category Members." *Memory & Cognition* 42, no. 7 (2014): 1011–25.
Marshall, Elizabeth. "Borderline Girlhoods: Mental Illness, Adolescence, and Femininity in Girl, Interrupted." *The Lion And The Unicorn* no. 1 (2006): 117. *Project MUSE*, EBSCO*host* (accessed May 19, 2015).
Mary and Max, dir. Adam Elliot. 2010; Melbourne Australia: Melodrama Pictures, 2010. DVD.
Memento, dir. Christopher Nolan. 2001; Santa Monica, CA: Summit Entertainment.
"Mentalhealth.gov," U.S. Department of Health and Human Services, April 22, 2018. https://www.mentalhealth.gov/basics/mental-health-myths-facts.
Monster, dir. Patty Jenkins. 2003; Los Angeles, CA: DEJ Productions, 2004. DVD.
Mozart and the Whale, dir. Petter Naess. 2005; New York: Big City Pictures, 2007. DVD.
Murray, Stuart. *Representing Autism: Culture, Narrative, Fascination.* Liverpool: Liverpool University Press, 2008.

North by Northwest, dir. Alfred Hitchcock. 1959; Culver City, California: Metro-Goldwyn-Mayer.
O'Brien, Gabrielle. "Mirror, Mirror: Fractured Female Identity in Black Swan." *Screen Education* no. 75 (2014): 102.
One Flew over the Cuckoo's Nest, dir. Miloš Forman. 1975; Berkeley, CA: Fantasy Films.
Pearson, Kyra. "The Trouble with Aileen Wuornos, Feminism's "First Serial Killer." *Communication & Critical/Cultural Studies* 4, no. 3 (2001): 256–75.
Phillips, Kendall R. "Consuming Community in Jonathan Demme's *The Silence of the Lambs.*" *Qualitative Research Reports in Communication* 1, no. 2 (2000): 26–32.
Plantinga, Carl R. *Moving Viewers: American Film and the Spectator's Experience.* Berkeley, CA: University of California Press, 2009.
Radio, dir. Michael Tollin. 2003; Santa Monica, CA: Revolution Studios, 2003. DVD.
Rain Man, dir. by Barry Levinson. 1988; Santa Monica, CA: MGM Home Entertainment, 2011. DVD.
Ratto, Casey M. "Not Superhero Accessible: The Temporal Stickiness of Disability in Superhero Comics." *Disability Studies Quarterly* 37, no. 2 (2017): 7.
Robb, Jayci, and Jeff Stone. "Implicit Bias toward People with Mental Illness: A Systematic Literature Review." *Journal of Rehabilitation* 82, no. 4 (2016): 3–13. *CINAHL Complete,* EBSCO*host* (accessed April 22, 2018).
Schultz, Jaime. "Glory Road (2006) and the White Savior Historical Sport Film." *Journal of Popular Film & Television* 42, no. 4 (October 2014): 205–13.
Scorpion, dir. Sam Hill. 2014–2018; Los Angeles, CA: CBS Television Studios.
Shutter Island, dir. Martin Scorsese. 2010; Hollywood, CA: Paramount Pictures.
Siebers, Tobin. *Disability Theory.* Ann Arbor, MI: University of Michigan Press, 2008.
Silence of the Lambs, The, dir. Johnathan Demme. 1991; Los Angeles, CA: Orion Pictures, 2001. DVD.
Simpson, J. C. and P. E. Cole. "Out of the Celluloid Closet." *Time* 139, no. 14 (1992): 65.
Smith, Murray. *Engaging Characters: Fiction, Emotion and the Cinema.* New York: Oxford University Press, 1995.
Soloist, The, dir. Joe Wright. 2009; Glendale, CA: Universal, 2009. DVD.
Sopranos, The, dir. Allen Coulter. 2008; New York: HBO Home.
Stout, Patricia A., Jorge Villegas, and Nancy A. Jennings. "Images of Mental Illness in the Media: Identifying Gaps in the Research." *Schizophrenia Bulletin* 30 (January 1, 2004): 543–61. *ScienceDirect,* EBSCO*host* (accessed August 29, 2016).
Sucker Punch, dir. Zack Snyder. 2011; Burbank, CA: Warner Brothers Entertainment.
Sunset Boulevard, dir. Billy Wilder. 1950; Hollywood, CA: Paramount Pictures, 2002. DVD.
Ta, Lynn, M., "Hurt So Good: Fight Club, Masculine Violence, and the Crisis of Capitalism." *Journal of American Culture,* no. 3 (2006): 265–77.
Temple Grandin, dir. Mick Jackson. 2010; Santa Monica, CA: HBO Films.
Thomson, Rosemarie Garland. *Extraordinary Bodies: Figuring Physical Disability in American Culture and Literature.* New York: Columbia University Press, 1997.
Top Gun, dir. Tony Scott. 1986; Hollywood, CA: Paramount Home Entertainment, 2011. DVD.
Treffert, Darold. "Savant Syndrome: Realities, Myths and Misconceptions." *Journal of Autism & Developmental Disorders,* 44, no. 3 (2014): 564–71.
What's Eating Gilbert Grape, dir. Lasse Hallström. 1993; Hollywood, CA: Paramount Pictures, 2013. DVD.
Wizard, The, dir. Todd Holland. 1990; Los Angeles, CA: The Finnegan/Pinchuk Company.

Index

12 Monkeys, 9, 69–83

A Beautiful Mind, 12, 15, 17
Abramsom, Kate, 69
Adam, 6
Afra, Kia, 5
anorexia, 17, 18, 25
antisocial personality disorder, 1, 3, 7, 30, 34–35, 37
Asperger syndrome. *See* autism spectrum disorder
autism spectrum disorder, 1, 4, 8, 41–53, 85
Ayers, Nathaniel Ayers, 56, 62–66

Babbitt, Charlie, 42–49, 53
Babbitt, Raymond, 8, 41–53, 55, 60
Bale, Christian, 31
Batman, 8, 30–33
Beauvior, Simone de, 5
Bill, Buffalo. *See* Jame Gumb
Black Swan, 3, 7, 11–27
Black, Gregory D., 5
Black, Rhonda S., 8, 49, 53, 55, 57–62, 65
blackface, 61
body dysmorphic disorder, 17, 18, 25, 26
borderline personality disorder, 1, 71, 73–74
Browning, Emily, 20
bulimia, 17, 18, 25
Butler, Judith, 11–12

capitalism, 4, 11, 12–15, 20, 26, 85–86
Carter, Helena Bonham, 20
Chopin, Kate, 85
class, 36
cognitive studies, 41–52
Cole, James, 79–83
communicable, 33

congenital mental disorders. *See* developmental disorder
consumerism. *See* capitalism
contagion, 29, 33, 70
Cross, Simon, 3, 4
Cruise, Tom, 42, 46
cultural capital, 34, 35, 38

Dark Knight, The, 7, 29–39
delusions, 21, 23, 24
Demme, Jonathan, 34
depression, 14
developmental disorder, 1, 3
Diagnostic and Statistical Manual of Mental Disorders 5, 1, 15, 18, 25, 26, 30, 71, 72–74
Dinkle, Mary Daisy, 50, 52
disability theory, 2
Discipline and Punish, 9, 70, 80
discourse of pity, 8, 53, 55, 57
dissociative identity disorder, 1, 11, 14–15, 21–22
Downey, Robert Jr., 56, 62
DSM-5. *See Diagnostic and Statistical Manual of Mental Disorders 5*
Durden, Tyler, 14–15, 20–21, 23–26, 44

Elliot, Adam, 50
engagement, 8, 41, 43–52, 50
Engaging Characters, 43
epistemology, 9, 70–71
exceptionalism, 41
Extraordinary Bodies: Figuring Physical Disability in American Culture and Literature, 1

femme fatale, 25, 38–39, 73–74, 78, 86
Fight Club, 3, 4, 7, 11–27, 44, 82, 86
Fisher, Mark, 23
Foster, Jodie, 34

Foucault, Michel, 9, 58, 70–71, 75–78, 80, 82
Foxx, Jamie, 56, 65

Gaslight, 69
gaslight, 9, 69–70
Gatens, Moira, 5
gender theory, 2, 7
Gilliam, Terry, 69, 79
"Girl Interrupted at Her Music," 74
Girl, Interrupted (book), 71, 74, 78
Girl, Interrupted (film), 9, 69–83
Giroux, Henry, 14
Goines, Jeffrey, 70
Gooding, Cuba Jr., 41, 56
Gothika, 82
Gumb, Jame, 30–31, 34–35, 39, 56
Gyllenhaal, Maggie, 33

Harper, Stephen, 3–4
Harris, Ed, 58
Hays Codes, 5–6, 37
Hays, Michael T., 8, 49, 53, 55, 57–62, 65
Hershey, Barbara, 17
Hoffman, Dustin, 41, 46, 61
Hoffman, Philip Seymour, 42, 50
Hollywood Censored: Morality Codes Catholics, and the Movies, 5
Hopkins, Anthony, 34, 35
Horovitz, Max Jerry, 42, 44, 50–53
Hughey, Mathew, 57

identification. *See* engagement

Jack, 7, 12–18, 20, 23–27, 44
Jacobs, Amber, 19
James Robert "Radio" Kennedy. *See* Radio
Jennings, Nancy A., 9, 69
Johnson, Mark, 49, 52
Joker, The, 7–8, 30–35, 36, 37, 39
Jolie, Angelina, 73

Kaysen, Susanna, 71, 74
Kellner, Douglass, 38

La Jetée, 79
Lecter, Hannibal, 8, 30, 34–39, 48, 56
Ledger, Heath, 31

Levine Ted, 34
Lopez, Steve, 56, 62–66
Lukin, Josh, 56–57

Madness, Power, and the Media: Class, Gender and Race in Popular Representations of Mental Distress, 3
magical negro, 57
makeup, 32, 33, 36
male gaze, 20, 23
Mangold, James, 69
Marshall, Elizabeth, 74
Mary and Max, 8, 41–54
masculinity, 4
mask, 32
masochism, 24
Mediating Madness: Mental Distress and Cultural Representation, 3
Memento, 12, 22
Monster, 30
Motion Picture Association of America. *See* Hays Codes
Motion Picture Producers and Distributers of America. *See* Hays Codes
Mozart and the Whale, 6
MPAA. *See* Hays Codes
MPPDA. *See* Hays Codes
multiple personality disorder. *See* dissociative personality disorder
Murray, Stuart, 4

Nicholson, Jack, 72
noble savage, 57
Nolan, Christopher, 31
normate, 1
Norton, Edward, 12

O'Brien, Gabrielle, 21
obsessive-compulsive disorder, 18
One Flew Over the Cuckoo's Next, 72
Other, 5–6, 8, 29, 30, 31, 38–39, 46, 55, 62, 66, 70, 86

panopticon, 75, 76, 80, 81–82
Passionate Views: Film Cognition, and Emotion, 48
PCA. *See* Hays Codes
Peek, Kim, 46

performative, 12
Pitt, Brad, 14, 15, 79
Plantinga, Carl, 48
post-traumatic stress disorder, 32
Production Code Administration. *See* Hays Codes
psychoanalysis, 43
psychopathy. *See* antisocial personality disorder
psychotic disorders, 1, 23, 63, 79, 80, 81, 82
Pulp Fiction, 47

Radio, 7, 8
Radio, 7–8, 41, 49, 55–66, 86
Railly, Kathryn, 79
Rain Man, 4, 7–8, 41–53, 56, 60–61, 85, 86
Representing Autism: Culture, Narrative, Fascination, 4
Robb, Jayci, 1, 34
Ryder, Winona, 16, 71

Sayers, Nina, 7, 12, 15–27
schizophrenia. *See* psychotic disorders
Schultz, Jamie, 55, 59
self-injury, 24–26
serial killer, 30, 34
Shutter Island, 12, 17
Siebers, Tobin, 59–62
Silence of the Lambs, 7–8, 29–39, 48, 52, 69
Smith, Greg M., 48
Smith, Murray, 8, 42, 43–50, 48, 49, 51, 53
sociopathy. *See* antisocial personality disorder
Soloist, The, 7–9, 49, 55–66, 86

Starling, Clarice, 34–35, 38
Stone, Jeff, 1, 34
"Storm, The," 85
Stout, Patricia A., 9, 69
Stowe, Madeline, 79
Sucker Punch, 12, 15, 20, 27
supercripple, 60
Swan Lake, 17

Ta, Lynn M., 12
The Cabinet of Dr. Caligari, 11, 12
The Dark Knight, 7, 8, 30
The Good Doctor, 6
The Second Sex, 5
The Secret Life of Bees, 57
Thomson, Rosemarie Garland, 1, 58–59
Tollin, Michael, 55, 58
transgendered, 38
trauma, 32

U.S. Department of Health and Human Services, 29
Undoing Gender, 12

Vermeer, Johannes, 74
vilify, 7
Villegas, Jorge, 9, 69
virgin-whore dichotomy, 16, 17, 18–19, 22–23, 25, 27

Wayne, Bruce. *See* Batman
white savior, 8, 55, 59, 66, 86
Whitmore, Bethany, 50
Willis, Bruce, 79
Wizard of Oz, 77
Wright, 55
Wuornos, Aileen, 30

About the Author

Originally from Odessa, Texas, **Erin Heath** received her bachelor's and master's degrees from Texas Tech University. She earned a PhD in English literature with minors in cinema and media studies and also gender and women's studies from the University of Illinois at Urbana-Champaign. She currently lives and works in Plainview, Texas. She is an associate professor in the Languages and Literature Department of Wayland Baptist University. She spends as much time as possible with her parents, grandmother, sisters, and nieces, and she lives companionably with her all-American dog, Emma.

Made in the USA
Las Vegas, NV
09 June 2021